JÖRG SAND

The Mercedes-Benz G-Class

The Complete History of an Off-Road Classic

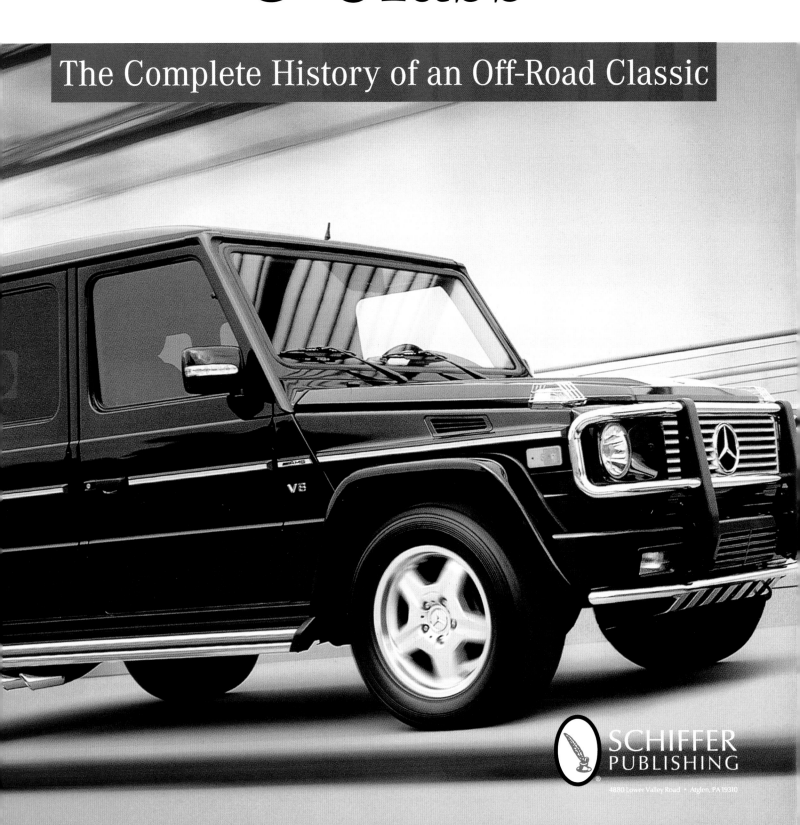

SCHIFFER PUBLISHING

4880 Lower Valley Road • Atglen, PA 19310

Cover design by Danielle D. Farmer
Type set in Corporate A/Domus

ISBN: 978-0-7643-6263-7
Printed in Serbia

Published by Schiffer Publishing, Ltd.
4880 Lower Valley Road
Atglen, PA 19310
Phone: (610) 593-1777; Fax: (610) 593-2002
E-mail: Info@schifferbooks.com
Web: www.schifferbooks.com

For our complete selection of fine books on this and related subjects, please visit our website at www.schifferbooks.com. You may also write for a free catalog.

Schiffer Publishing's titles are available at special discounts for bulk purchases for sales promotions or premiums. Special editions, including personalized covers, corporate imprints, and excerpts, can be created in large quantities for special needs. For more information, contact the publisher.

We are always looking for people to write books on new and related subjects. If you have an idea for a book, please contact us at proposals@schifferbooks.com.

Contents

Foreword

Hello, Mercedes G-Class Friends!

The Mercedes G celebrated its fortieth production anniversary in 2019, making it the longest-serving vehicle ever built by Daimler. A lot has happened concerning the G-Class since the first edition of this book in 2005. In 2006, there was speculation that the G—or "G-Wagen" in the United States and United Kingdom—would be discontinued, because, in fact, with the GL an apparently similar product had come on the market. After a profitability audit, Daimler decided in favor of continuing to manufacture the civilian G model because, as it turned out, this vehicle has the highest profit margin per unit in the brand's entire product range. The military version, in any event, would not have been affected by the production stop anyway, because the supply contracts with the military include a ten-year follow-up delivery capability for the procured vehicles. Thus, the German armed forces, the Bundeswehr, also took delivery of the vehicles in 2018, which means that production of the G will continue at least until 2028.

The G-Class is exactly ten years younger than I am, but it doesn't look its age. It is hard to say what it is about this vehicle that has made me warm to it so much—maybe because I made my first attempt at driving at the age of fourteen in a 230 GE, or because my 300 GD has never let me down. Basically, it is probably because I can always get enthusiastic about things that are built to last: a Swiss watch, everyday items made of stainless steel, or other masterpieces of craftsmanship. In the age of the throwaway society, I enjoy things that are of lasting value and maintain continuity.

The G radiates all of this, even if this isn't obvious to everyone. It stubbornly resists superficial changes, remains true to its line, and accepts only those innovations that are necessary and reasonable. Built like a castle, it bristles with its robust quality in the face of fast-living times, confident in the knowledge that as long as extreme demands are still made on automobiles, its continued existence is ensured. It is a guy with rough edges, but it wants to be spoiled. It drinks more than others, and its technology demands regular maintenance. If you stick with it, as an owner you will have a companion who never lets you down. Even if you get bored by the G because you are driving it only on the street, it won't take it amiss. It gives its drivers the feeling that they can do so much more than anyone else involved in the traffic flow. The G is built for extreme conditions and for military use, as well as for driving in undeveloped areas. Most G-Wagen drivers will not push their vehicle to the limit. But the G is well prepared for any eventuality. With the introduction of the W 463 A in 2018, the history of the G-Class will continue to be written. Although the successor is designed much more for luxury and comfort, it retains a large part of the genes of the original G. Its sales success confirms the unbroken fascination with this vehicle. The traditional range of engines, from the turbo diesel to the 500 and beyond to the AMG, will be retained, and for the military, the W 461 remains in the product range.

I wish you an enjoyable read.

Jörg Sand
Troisdorf, Spring 2019

Paul Graetz while crossing
southern Africa

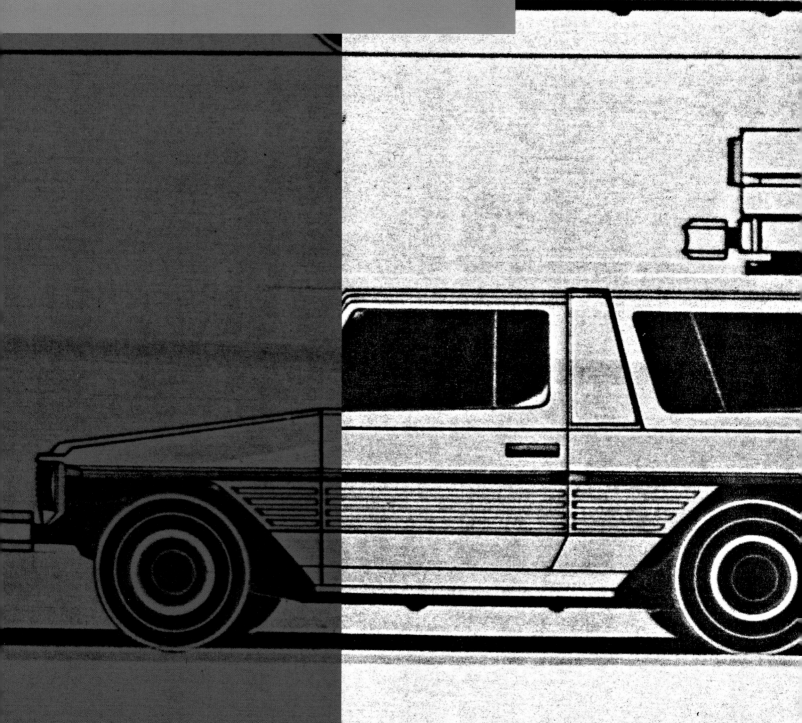

1. History and Development of a Classic

This is the Dernburg car. Daimler produced a 1:8 model for the Detroit Motor Show in 2007 to mark the anniversary of "100 years of all-wheel drive." The car has been considered forgotten since 1915.

The Prehistory of the Mercedes G-Class

Paul Graetz while crossing southern Africa

The Prehistory of the Mercedes G-Class

The Graetz Spezial — The early ancestors of the G-Class can be found as early as 1907. At that time, German officer Paul Graetz commissioned Süddeutsche Automobilfabrik in Gaggenau (a forerunner of the Mercedes-Benz plant where the Unimog was later made) to build him a car for driving across Africa. The two-wheel-drive special vehicle was based on a bus chassis and had 35 cm ground clearance. Graetz started his trip across Africa on August 10, 1907, in Dar es Salaam, Tanzania, and he reached his destination in Swakopmund, Namibia, on May 1, 1909. The Graetz Special was the first car to drive across Africa.

The Dernburg Car — An all-wheel-drive vehicle, the so-called Dernburg car, was also built by Daimler Motoren AG in 1907. Its owner was the minister of state of the German Reich Colonial Office, Bernhard Dernburg. This car was the first all-wheel-drive car in the world that was powered by a gasoline engine. The Dernburg car was a Daimler with an open touring-car body, weighed 3.6 tons, and had all-wheel steering. It was used by the police force in German South West Africa (now Namibia).

The German *Allgemeine Auto Zeitung* (*AAZ*) (General Auto Newspaper) wrote in 1908: "The Dernburg-Wagen is the term used for an off-road vehicle that the Daimler Motoren Gesellschaft (DMG) built in 1907 as a 'colonial wagon' on behalf of the Reich Colonial Office, which His Excellency Secretary of State Dernburg will use on his trip to our West African colonies. The car is equipped with four-wheel drive."

The car was made at the Daimler plant in Berlin-Marienfelde. The car had a wheelbase of 4 meters (m) and had a 6.9-liter, four-cylinder engine. At 800 revolutions per minute, the maximum speed was 40

km/h. Fuel consumption was given as 23 kg of gasoline per 100 km. The heavy weight of the vehicle often led to tire damage when it was driven in Africa. During its first 10,000 kilometers (km) in what was then German South West Africa, the Dernburg car wore out thirty-six tires and twenty-seven tubes, according to the historical travel logbook.

The G1 and G2 — In 1926, in the year when Daimler and Benz merged to become Daimler-Benz AG, the history of the Mercedes-Benz off-road vehicle began with the G1 test vehicle. The car was made on demand; high-level off-road mobility was required. At that time, it was thought that this could be achieved only with a three-axle design. However, the prototype of the G1 (W 103) was defeated in the tender by a comparable vehicle from Horch. It was a three-axle off-road passenger vehicle, equipped with a 3.0-liter, six-cylinder, in-line gasoline engine (M 03) that delivered 50 hp. On the G1, only the two rear axles were driven. The rigid axles were steered on leaf springs.

The G2 followed in 1927; except for the details, it was a lengthened version of the G1. The G2 got a modified engine with an engine displacement of 3,100 cubic centimeters (ccm) and 58 hp. The G2 also has an integrated winch. Only seven vehicles in all of the G1 and G2 models were ever built.

The G3 — The 1928 G3 was likewise the three-axle successor to the G2 and was also powered by six-cylinder engines. The G3 was presented with an increased 3.5-liter engine displacement and 60 hp, followed by a version with a 4.1-liter diesel engine and 63 hp. In total, only eighty-nine of the model G1 to G3 series were produced.

The G3a followed in 1929, and the vehicle, which had improved in many respects, was often sold with a truck superstructure.

The six-cylinder engine of the G3a had a displacement of 3.7 liters and performed at 68 hp. The model G3a series already has limited slip differentials on both drive axles. Mercedes sold 2,000 units until 1935, most of which were used by the Wehrmacht—the armed forces of the German Third Reich—up until the Second World War.

In 1929, a completely new off-road vehicle came from Mercedes, the Stuttgart military utility vehicle model. The two-axle Stuttgart had selectable front-wheel drive and was specially designed for the Reichswehr, the armed forces of the Weimar Republic.

The G4 — The G 500 (G4), model name W 31, from 1933, outclassed all other off-road vehicles of the time in terms of size and comfort. This luxury off-road vehicle was powered by a powerful 5.0-liter, eight-cylinder, in-line engine (M 24). The engine came from the passenger car model series of the time. The heavy unit generated 100 hp at 3,400 rpm. With its huge dimensions, this powerful three-axle car surpassed almost all contemporaneous cars. The G4 models also had manually lockable differentials on both drive axles (rear) (100% locking ratio).

In 1934, the G 500 was followed by the G 520 (G4). In the G 520, not only was the engine displacement increased to 5.2 liters, but there was another innovation that was even more important. With the 520, the early G-Class gained all-wheel drive (6×6). However, the six driven wheels had to carry a total weight of 3.5 tons over the terrain. Armored versions of the G4 easily put 4.4 tons on the scales. The performance, increased to 115 hp, allowed a top speed of 70 km/h. In addition to the locking differentials on the two rear axles, it was also possible to order one for the driven front axle on request. The model G4 series was produced as an eight-seat, open passenger car; a closed station wagon; or an armored vehicle. The dimensions of the

Left: A G3a of the Deutsche Reichsbahn (German national railroad), late 1920s

Right: By the 1930s, the axle articulation that could be attained was remarkable.

13

Left: The G4 had an extremely stable ladder frame.

Right: Depending on the customer, G4 series vehicles featured different details, such as different fenders.

G4 were gigantic: 5.36 m (G 500: 5.18 m) long, 1.86 m wide, and 1.90 m high. The biggest customers for the G4 were the German Reichspost (Post Office) and the Reich Chancellery in Berlin. While the Reichspost used the station wagon version mainly as a telecommunications vehicle, the Reich Chancellery used the G4 as its parade vehicle.

The Reich Chancellery ordered four more luxurious G 540s (G4) for the same purpose in 1936. These mighty vehicles were perfect and impressive in every respect. The G 540 and G 520 were identical, except in terms of the engine displacement. The silky-smooth running of the large-volume eight-cylinder engine made it possible to travel in a previously unknown level of comfort. The four vehicles went to Adolf Hitler, Hermann Göring, Benito Mussolini, and Francisco Franco. Franco's G 540 is still kept in perfect condition and can be viewed in the El Prado de Madrid carriage house. Franco used his G 540 primarily for hunting, so the vehicle displays a very low mileage of 19,000 km. The car was given a complete overhaul at the Mercedes Classic Center in Fellbach in 2004. Only fifty-seven cars of the model G4 (W 31) series were produced in all. By 1942 there were plans for a successor to the G4. The vehicle was in fact supposed to become even bigger, but it had to make do with two axles.

The 170 VG — From 1935 to 1936, Mercedes-Benz produced the 170 VG (W 133 III) and 170 VL (W 139) SUVs. The all-wheel-drive military utility vehicle, based on the Mercedes 170 V with a 1.7-liter, four-cylinder engine (M 136 MIL) and 38 hp, offered very little comfort but very good off-road driving features. Due to its all-wheel steering, the 170 VL had a sensationally small turning circle of only 7 m. Mercedes-Benz sold 100 of the 104 vehicles it produced to the German Wehrmacht.

The G5 — The G5 was built from 1937 until 1941. It was not, as the name suggests, the successor to the G4, but rather a new design that replaced the 170 VG. The G5 had four-wheel drive and four-wheel steering. It was powered by a 2.0-liter, four-cylinder gasoline engine with 45 hp. Some 606 units of this so-called "colonial" car were manufactured. The German Wehrmacht alone received 378 units of the model G5 convertible command vehicle. The German Bergwacht—the Mountain Rescue Service—was the second-largest buyer of this extreme off-road car. The remaining buyers, the large number of private customers, who used the G5 as a hunting or expedition car, made it into the first civilian off-road vehicle in the world. The G5 was presented as a "colonial car" at the London Motor Show in 1938 and was an absolute innovator at the time. Besides the all-wheel drive and four-wheel steering, it made a convincing impression with its good chassis and small overhangs when driving off-road. In its time, the Mercedes-Benz G5 was out in front of the other vehicles in its class in terms of off-road mobility. The G5 (W 152) was available in three vehicle body styles, as a military utility vehicle for the Wehrmacht, as a simple military utility vehicle without doors for the police and Mountain Rescue Service, and as a comfortable touring car for private drivers.

L 1500 A — From 1941 to 1943, Mercedes built the model L 1500 A (L 301) military personnel car. Daimler-Benz delivered 4,900 units of this all-wheel-drive vehicle to the Wehrmacht. The vehicle load capacity was up to 1,500 kg, and the permissible total weight was 4,100 kg. The vehicle was powered by a 2.6-liter, in-line, six-cylinder engine (M 159). The engine generated 60 hp at 3,000 rpm. The L 1500 A reached a top speed of 85 km/h on the road and consumed 19 liters of gasoline per 100 km. This car had a selectable all-wheel drive and two locking differentials.

Left: Here is a military utility model 170 VG with all-wheel steering.

Right: The military utility G5 model also had to prove its capabilities in the Bergwacht (Mountain Rescue Service).

Left: Universal motor machine: versatility is the great strength of the Unimog (*Universal-Motor-Gerät* or universal engine).

Right: The Austrian ancestor named Haflinger also has sensational off-road mobility.

The Unimog — The Mercedes Unimog can also be counted among the ancestors of the G-Wagen; it originated in 1946 from a compulsory plan that was conceived for Germany. After the Second World War, Germany was to be restructured into an agricultural state in accordance with the first Allied plans (the Morgenthau Plan). Production of capital goods that could be used for military purposes was initially banned. The director of Mercedes-Benz aircraft engine development then came up with the idea of the Unimog, a vehicle that had the capabilities of a truck, although it was actually a tractor. The Universal-Motor-Gerät was initially intended for purely agricultural use. The American military occupying power approved the production of this agricultural machine in 1946. Until 1951, the Unimog was built by the Boehringer company (a tractor factory), using Mercedes parts. Mercedes-Benz took over production starting in 1951. At the time, the military was particularly keen on the Unimog, with its versatile deployment capability. The Swiss army had already started ordering Unimogs in 1951. As a result, the army customers from many countries developed into a established sales figure for the corporation. The military particularly values reliability, robustness, and unbeatable off-road mobility. The Unimog S 404 model and its successors, which were specially developed for armies, are still the benchmark for wheel-driven off-road vehicles. Unimogs are used all over the world today for the widest range of potential purposes.

"G" Stands for Geländewagen ("Off-Road Vehicle," or SUV)

In terms of their purpose, *Geländewagen* (or SUVs) are actually utility vehicles, and this is how they are conceptualized in general. In today's world, where advertisers have skillfully associated the myth of independence and individualism, coupled with a

15

an SUV requires, and proves itself to be all the more superior as the requirement profile grows.

There are only a few "highly off-road mobile" vehicles that can be driven over sand dunes, along riverbeds, in deep mud, and in the high mountains without being dependent on access to roads and paths. In the huge fleet of the so-called SUVs, there is only a handful left that have these capabilities. The Mercedes G is one of them. Because it is very roadworthy for an SUV, it has set standards in this vehicle segment on the basis of the totality of its features, which are still valid today.

It has pushed back the boundaries of driving comfort and off-road mobility. In terms of directional stability and steering behavior, the Mercedes G had already surpassed its competitor, the Range Rover, by far when it first appeared in 1979. The G-Wagen is "multicultural." The G gets half of its genes not from Mercedes, but from Austria. Its ancestors include the Puch Haflinger and the Puch Pinzgauer. In terms of the Pinzgauer, the relationship is also documented by means of some identical or similar components (rims, switches, door handles). Many critics today describe the G-Class as an anachronism; most so-called SUVs could also master 90 percent of the routes that a G can manage. But the remaining 10 percent show the true strengths of the G-Class.

Development of the Mercedes G-Class

In 1979, the expectations for the SUV from Mercedes were high; it should be nothing less than the best SUV in the world. The utility vehicle department of Daimler-Benz was entrusted with the implementation of the project. The development history of this unique vehicle took an incredible seven years. The G was to be better suited for off-road use than all the Jeeps and Land Rovers, while being as comfortable and safe on the road as a passenger car. While the G's Puch predecessors (Haflinger and Pinzgauer) made their way along extravagant special paths with portal and swing axles and can also be clearly assigned to the utility vehicle sector, the G was primarily intended to orient toward a different kind of vehicle. During the G development period, there was a vehicle already on the market that had revolutionized the SUV market significantly.

The Range Rover, presented in 1970, can certainly be seen as a template for the development of the G. The suspension system of the Mercedes Unimog, with rigid axles on coil springs, had already been successfully

During the first studies, the project was given the designation "H II," which stood for "Haflinger II."

flair for freedom and adventure, with the class of the SUVs, in a car world that has become boring and uniform, these jacks-of-all-trades, however, have often seen more of the big-city jungle than of the wilderness in the real jungle.

In fact, an SUV not only should be a fashionable car for everyday use, but, according to its name, should above all be able to drive where the roads end and the rough terrain begins. In contrast to most vehicles that even many automotive journalists count as SUVs, the Mercedes G really lives up to this name. The Mercedes G-Class combines all the qualities that

The designers of the G model had to meet many requirements.

Below: The design of the W 460 retains its timeless quality up to the present.

copied in the Range Rover and was later used in the G as well. The Range Rover was anything but perfect in terms of build quality, drive, and overall solidity, but the philosophy of creating an SUV suitable for everyday use showed clear potential for the future. A car of superlatives was created: there had never been any vehicle like the Mercedes G before. Development began in 1972 with the cooperation agreement between the German Daimler Benz AG and the Austrian Steyr-Daimler-Puch AG. The goal was to develop an all-wheel-drive SUV for private users. There was already abundant technical competence at Mercedes-Benz due to the Unimog model series and the production of four-wheel-drive trucks, but they decided to cooperate with Steyr-Daimler-Puch anyway.

The Austrian company, based in Graz, also had a high-quality SUV in its model range (the Puch

By means of sometimes-quite-daring style studies, they ultimately found the way to a classic design.

Pinzgauer), and it also had a great deal of know-how available in this vehicle class. Mercedes-Benz and Steyr-Daimler-Puch founded a joint company specifically for production of the G model, the Geländefahrzeuggesellschaft (GFG; Off-Road Vehicle Company). Graz was likewise headquartered in the Austrian state of Styria, where a completely new assembly hall was then built for production of the Mercedes G-Class. Development started in 1973 with the first wooden model. A year later, test drives were done with the first prototype. It was clear from the beginning that the vehicle would become an uncompromising "conqueror of all before it." For this reason, it was decided to use two complex 100 percent locking differentials for the drive system, with a fully

synchronized transfer case as another special feature. With the final decision to start series production in 1975, the comfort familiar from passenger cars was added to the specifications for the G-Class, in addition to high-quality off-road mobility. The biggest challenge at the time was to give the robust rigid-axle chassis the capability for proper road handling, which was almost impossible in the view of many experts. The development team solved the problem by precisely guiding the stable axles on large trailing arms and wishbone transverse control arms and by using coil springs instead of the leaf springs commonly used at the time. In addition, a stabilizer for the front axle was installed. This balanced construction remained up to date until the W 463.

The heavy bumpers
and wheels are a bit
reminiscent of a buggy.

Except for the angular
headlights, this design
is already a lot like the
series production.

19

The car body was changed only slightly during the first forty years of production.

Passenger cars that had a limited capability to drive off-road were already available for sale. There were also already properly roadworthy all-terrain vehicles. But these compromises were not acceptable to Mercedes-Benz. In seven years of scientific development work, the G was created as a vehicle that has high-quality off-road mobility and is fully roadworthy.

The development work was focused on function; the logic of creating a well-thought-out off-road vehicle enjoyed the highest priority from the very beginning. The Mercedes off-road vehicle was intended to satisfy both civilian and military customers. Not an easy task, since the balancing act between the demands seemed almost unattainable—on the one hand, the military, which placed the emphasis on high-quality off-road mobility and immense robustness (after all, military off-road vehicles must be able to follow tracked vehicles off-road), and on the other hand, the civilian market, which above all demanded comfort and roadworthiness. The G-Class was the answer to all of these demands in every respect.

The test drives used on the G-Class represent an endurance test for material stress that probably is unique even today. Seldom has a vehicle been so thoroughly tested. For practical testing of the G-Class prototypes, the development team chose extreme test routes. Part of the off-road testing took place on the

huge strip-mining area of Rheinbraun AG between Cologne and Aachen. There, the G models had to show what they were made of on sand and rubble, in water and mud, and through steep breakneck passes. G models were tested in the Alps at the same time. The G covered thousands of kilometers just on the 1,450 m high Schöckl Mountain alone, the "home" mountain of Steyr-Daimler-Puch.

A G-Wagen had to endure 15,000 km of continuous use on the Schöckl, after which a thorough inspection was required. All off-road vehicles that were driven on the Schöckl for comparison were already "totaled" (frame breakage) after 10,000 km. In North Africa, Argentina, Arabia, and Turkey, and within the polar circle as well, the G prototypes traveled endless kilometers for testing.

In parallel, driving-dynamics tests were conducted on roads and test tracks. To give the G models irreproachable road handling, complex fine-tuning of suspension and damping was needed. The result of this development was a vehicle that feels just as comfortable in the city and on the highway as it does in the Sahara, in the mud, or in the high mountains. The G-Class also boasted high load capacities and trailer loads. The design followed the rule "Form follows function." And it is precisely this unmistakably uncompromising bodywork, designed for off-road

Photos of the first prototype: chief designer Bruno Sacco didn't want to send the G out on the street in a design that was too "angular." For safety reasons, the G was equipped with a rollover bar, while the half doors were reserved for the military versions.

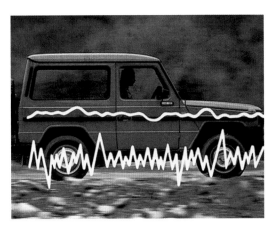

use, that still accounts for the unique character of the Mercedes G model today.

Series production began on February 10, 1979, and the Mercedes off-road vehicle was given its first public presentation during the same month on the Paul Ricard racetrack in southern France. Five body versions, two wheelbases, and four engines were available at that time.

Daimler-Benz and Steyr-Daimler-Puch founded the Geländefahrzeug-Gesellschaft (GFG) in 1977 to build the Mercedes/Puch G. The divorce came already by 1981. In the September issue of *Off-Road* magazine, you could read that "the Daimlers from Sindelfingen and the Daimlers from Graz can't really work together any longer." Fortunately, G-Class production continued to run smoothly even in separated companies. Daimler announced that they had "agreed to reorganize cooperation in the development, production, and sale of the G model series of off-road vehicles. Thereafter, Daimler-Benz AG and Steyr-Daimler-Puch AG were to take over the further development of the off-road vehicles they each sell."

The same applied to sales. Vehicles with the "Puch" brand were destined for Austria, Switzerland, Yugoslavia, and the Comecon countries, while those with the "Daimler-Benz" brand were for all the other markets. In the end, things were not that bad, and the Puch G differed from the Mercedes G only in its nameplate.

Just as in the past, the G-Class vehicles are still largely built by hand in Graz, Austria, today. Since the 1982 model year, however, GFG has no longer been responsible for the production of the G, but instead Mercedes-Benz and Steyr-Daimler-Puch are each responsible for their own models. In 1987 the 50,000th G left the factory in Graz. In 1992 the 100,000th unit was produced. In 1999 the 150,000th unit of the model series was produced, and in 2017 the 300,000 unit was delivered. Right from the start, the G models for Switzerland, Austria, and the Eastern Bloc countries were sold under the "Puch" brand name.

The chassis subjected to a practical test (*above*), under simulated vibration (*middle*), and being tested for leakage in the sludge basin (*below*).

Handicraft remains a benchmark for quality in the production of the G models up to the present.

Manufacturing the
G-Class is pure
teamwork.

"Schöckl therapy": The W 463 A, still in
camouflage here, also had to climb the course
up Graz's home mountain.

The Mercedes G models accounted for a good 90 percent of production until 1996, and 10 percent were sold under the Puch-G name. All G models have been sold exclusively by Mercedes since the year 2000. At the beginning of the 1990s, production was distributed at 50 percent each between the G W 461 and W 463 models.

With an average of 7,500 vehicles produced each year, the G is anything but a mass-produced vehicle. The main reason for this is, above all, its extremely high price, which is explained by the complex production of the body and frame and the handicraft assembly process. Or, as it was one formulated by the press chief at the Puch company: "As it turned out, no kind of simple or even inexpensive solutions were the right choice for the G."

Mercedes-Benz established the G at a rank above the mass-produced products from Japan; in its price range, the Range Rover was its only competitor. As early as 1979, it was possible to buy a comparably powered S-Class for the price of a G-Class, and this hasn't changed until today. It has always been something special to drive one of the vehicles from Graz, one of those incredibly mobile masterpieces of modern off-road-vehicle technology. The Mercedes M-Class was later developed to conquer the SUV segment; this model has also held its own in this market and has now been replaced by the GLE.

The W 463 and W 461 had the world's most powerful all-wheel-drive system, thanks to continual model upgrading starting in 2001. With its unique combination of permanent all-wheel drive, the 4ETS electronic traction system and ESP, fully synchronized gear reduction, and three differential locks, the G-Class is truly up to any challenge. In addition, it offers typical Mercedes driving safety on the road.

Little has changed to this day, with one exception: with the introduction of the W 463 A in 2018, the G lost a unique selling point. Instead of the special

Before the G goes to its owner, manufacturing quality is checked extensively.

Left: Passenger protection has always been a strength of the G.

Right: The first prototypes looked a little tomboyish.

G-Class transfer case, the one already in use in GLE/GLS and X350d was to be installed. In contrast to the well-known VG150, the power is not conveyed by gear wheels on this, but via chains. On the road, the torque is not distributed 50:50, but 60 percent at the rear and 40 percent at the front. Thus, driving performance on the road is significantly improved.

Ener-G-Force

In December 2011, Daimler shocked G-Class fans with the "Ener-G-Force" design concept. This monstrous vehicle stood on 20-inch rims with heavily built 38-inch MT tires and had an integrated front winch, additional headlights, and a luggage rack. There were those who found this interpretation of how the genes of the 1979 off-road classic might have an impact on the future to be too radical. As we know today, the fear remained unfounded: The W 463 successor looks practically the same as the old version did. "The Ener-G-Force was rather a reference to the new off-road design from Mercedes-Benz," head of design Gorden Wagener stated. In retrospect, the study influenced all new Mercedes off-roaders, from the compact GLA to the pickup X-Class. The design of the Ener-G-Force is unmistakably based on the G-Class.

It also has a front end with an expressive radiator grill and integrated headlights. The LEDs in the headlights form G-shaped lighting units. The front

indicators are mounted on the wings, a significant G-Class element, like navigation lights. The attached roof, which is typical of the G-Class, and the three-part side window area also cite the original design of the classic. Behind what is supposed to be a spare-tire cover—which of course could never accommodate the model's Ferris wheel–sized tires, there is a tool compartment that can be opened using a lug wrench. Steps are integrated into the bumpers.

Study: The design concept for the 2011 Ener-G-Force is gigantic. Behind what is supposed to be a spare tire cover, which of course could never accommodate the model's giant tires, there is a tool compartment that can be opened using a lug wrench. Steps are integrated into the bumpers.

2. The G-Class Models

A glamorous entrance: The last W 463 series with a rigid front axle was built between 2015 and 2018. In addition, this G 500 has the new M 176 engine.

The 1980 range: the W 460 is available in long model, in short model, and as a panel van and open model.

Below, from left: Two W 463s, a civilian W 461, and a military W 461 can be seen.

The "original" G-Wagen is the W 460 with selectable all-wheel drive. It was manufactured from 1979 to 1991. The almost vertical exterior walls and the steeply slanted windshield created a unique interior volume and a sense of space like no other off-roader; in the Mercedes G, you are sitting upright above everyone else. In fact, even at its market launch in 1979, the G-Class body design was already considered to be rather "utility vehicle oriented." Despite constant improvements to the W 460, customers demanded even more comfort and performance, and an ABS-compatible all-wheel drive. To meet these requirements, Mercedes decided to develop the W 463 series. However, the W 460 remained in the model range in the form of the W 461, modified as a utility vehicle, although the differences between the two models in terms of body shape become apparent only in the area behind the B pillar. There is space for five passengers in the short G models, plus two more on the optional extra seats in the rear. In the long design, there was room for four people in the extra seats, so it could accommodate nine passengers.

The G (W 461), built from 1991 to 2001, is in principle identical to the W 460. In the W 461, only a few comfort features (carpet, electric windows, etc.) have been saved in comparison to the W 460. The utility vehicle model series featured exotic extras such as a tank nozzle that also works for filling canisters, and a "grass fire" protection package. However, the civilian versions of the W 461, which were very popular among long-distance travelers, were never produced in large numbers due to their high purchase prices.

The military version of the W 460/461 was built from 1979 to 2001. The extensive armament orders received from various countries at that time ensured that every second G left the production facilities in the camouflage paintwork design, making the G model economically the most successful military vehicle in its class.

Since 2003, the W 461 has been sold under the names "Green Line" (military) or "Professional" (civilian). The G 270 CDI, G 280 CDI, and G 300 CDI have the drive technology of the W 463 but are otherwise identical (body, equipment) to the W 461.

The W 461s (G 300 Professional) have not been available as new vehicles in the EU since 2017, due to the strict exhaust gas regulations for diesel vehicles.

There aren't many SUVs that can be used for climbing exercises like this—for the G, it's child's play.

33

Here is one of the first 280 GEs from 1979. These vehicles were delivered to the Bundesgrenzschutz (BGS), the German federal border guard. They have a roof hatch for one observer and seven seats.

Right side: A W 460 of the first model year in alpine surroundings

They remain available for military orders and for civilian markets outside the EU and the United States.

The W 462 is a W 461 that was assembled from 1992 to 1996 by the ELBO company in Thessaloniki, Greece; the unit number was 25,000, made from prefabricated CKD (completely knocked down) parts. The Mercedes parts used in the Peugeot P4, which is almost visually identical and was the result of a German-French military cooperation project, are also listed under the spare-part numbers of the W 462. All G models not assembled in Graz were given a vehicle identification number using 462. These also include the Panhard G models used by the special units of the French army, and the G 300 Professional models made in Algeria for the local police and army.

The vehicles were built for the Cypriot army at ELBO in Thessaloniki. These 240/250 and 290 GDs have right-hand drive and are still in use today.

The W 463, built from 1990 to 2018, is the Comfort series of the G-Class, and the electrical sliding roof, leather, and ABS were initially available only in this model. From a technical point of view, it was particularly important to quiet down the drivetrain, which was too noisy for many customers due to the wide flexion angles of the driveshafts. Development of the W 463 series started in 1987; by the autumn of 1989, the Comfort series had already been introduced. The decisive technical difference from the W 460 and W 461 is the W 463's permanent all-wheel drive. The W 463 can even drive with no strain in the gear reduction (with center open differential). This unique technical highlight makes completely neutral handling possible in the off-road gear reduction. The most striking change to the exterior on the W 463 is the front end, painted in the color of the body. But when looking at the interior, it becomes clear to everyone that the

W 463 is a different car. In comparison to the spartan W 460/461, the impact of the W 463 interior design, which has been adopted from the W-124 limousine, is almost luxurious.

The W 463 A, launched in 2018, is completely new and replaces the W 463. This evolution here is by far greater than the step from the W 460 to the W 463. The ladder frame, the rigid axle at the rear, and the body shape are practically all that remained; otherwise, everything is different. The mutation into something like a comfortable luxury liner is intentional. It has advantages and disadvantages. The W 463 A is a much-better normal road vehicle. Despite its larger size, however, it offers less utility value.

On the exterior, the W 463 A has become a bit rounder everywhere; inside, a completely new interior has moved in with opulent luxury features. The new front axle with independent wheel suspension makes it possible to install modern driver-assistance systems. In the W 463 A, you can barely trace any of the G utility vehicle's genes.

1979–2019

For clarification and understanding, we would like to point out that due to the fact that production plant vacations normally occur during August, in the automotive industry model changes always take place from August to September. A car model year therefore runs from the beginning of September to the end of August of the following year. Thus, the 1980 model year starts in September 1979. The specified year numbers always refer to the model years. The listed model changes include the standard features and optional features. To meet the extreme and differing demands of the wide range of G-Class buyers, there has always been an extensive and special list of optional extra features for the G-model series, so that every customer can put together his or her own totally individual vehicle.

W 460

1979

The G-Class entered its first model year in February 1979 as the 230 G, 280 GE, 240 GD, and 300 GD. The interior of the first G models (you can easily recognize them by the steering wheel) originates from the Mercedes-Benz van series. The horn on the first generation of G vehicles is still located on the multifunction lever and not on the steering wheel, and the windshield washer system is operated by a pump in the footwell. In terms of body design, the following models are available: short/open, short station wagon, and long station wagon. The vehicles from the first model year, from August 1979 to September 1980,

are available in only five colors (white, yellow, green, beige, and red). Almost all customers ordered the 100 percent locking differentials, which were initially available only as optional equipment. The upholstery is made of MB-Tex (synthetic leather) or tartan fabric (dark brown and black). The roof liner is available only in bamboo beige. Power steering is available only for a surcharge in the first model year of the four-cylinder 230 G and 240 GD; from the 1981 model onward, it was standard equipment on all versions of the G. Early W 460s have meanwhile become particularly sought after, since they can be inexpensively registered and insured as classic cars in many countries, including Germany. In Germany, there is also no environmental sticker requirement for such vehicles. The price trend shows that the G-Class has developed into a sought-after classic car. Thus, well-maintained or even restored 280 GE convertibles are being sold for more than 80,000 euros, and closed vehicles for over 70,000 euros.

1980
A closed panel van with a short or long wheelbase goes into series production.

1981

For the 1981 model year, the G was given new trailer couplings with a towing capacity of 2,800 kg (instead of 2,000 kg). Besides this, more optional features were made available. As a result, an automatic transmission, a hardtop (for the covered vehicle), a cable winch (from Rotzler), an under-chassis air-conditioning system (from Behr), an auxiliary drive (!), lengthwise seating in the loading space, and additional tanks (two of 13.5 liters each) all are now available. Furthermore, the selection of paintwork colors has now been expanded to a total of twenty-two. Starting in 1981, the G was also available with right-hand drive.

Large image above: The divided rear door and the colors are typical of the early G models.

Left side: Orders for the panel vans are very rare.

Below left: The first W 460s were very spartanly furnished; the plaid upholstered seats of the first generation are rare finds.

Below center: The combination coupling made it possible to use the G as a commercial towing vehicle.

Right: The tropical roof for driving in very hot regions

asten-Wagen, langer Radstand.

Offener Wagen, kurzer Radstand.

ation-Wagen, langer Radstand.

Station-Wagen, kurzer Radstand.

Left side: The Mercedes optional equipment range even includes a robust "Rotzler" cable winch.

1982

This year, the model range will be expanded to include the many civilian versions with either long or short wheelbase and folding windshield (it was possible to register such vehicles in Germany only with special approval). The GFG lettering was left off the front fenders. The interior is upgraded with steering-wheel and light switches taken from the passenger car series, as well as with new seat upholstery featuring small diamonds in brown, black, or gray.

1983

The 230 GE replaces the 230 G. The dashboard is now illuminated and the "sophisticated features" are standard. The range of optional extras is supplemented by stationary heating (from Webasto), Recaro seats, wide tires, aluminum rims (15 inch), and fender flares (made of FRP). For the first time, it is possible to order metallic paintwork.

1984

A five-speed gearbox from Getrag is available on the 230 GE, 280 GE, and 300 GD models. The dashboards are upgraded using soft plastic and illuminated switches, and the three-stage blower now has a rotary switch. The air-conditioning system, which is available as an optional extra, is now integrated into the ventilation system. Automatic transmission is available on the 230 GE.

1985

All 280 GE models are given an exhaust gas recirculation system due to new exhaust regulations and still generate 150 hp. On the open G, a more comfortable convertible top is now available in addition to the standard top. The convertible top is operated by using six gas pressure springs, and the cover fabric and the fasteners are from the Mercedes SL (R 107). A pickup version of the G-Class (with a long wheelbase) is also added to the range.

Superior on every terrain, sovereign on all roads.

This unique driving technology benefits the Mercedes G not only on rugged terrain, but also in all-around use on all roads.

For example, the all-wheel drive generally improves directional stability when driving fast around curves or in the rain, but especially in snow and on slippery roadways. The rigid axles and coil springs with extremely long spring deflection ensure that the vehicle is exceptionally easy to control, and not only off-road. This suspension technology also makes optimal handling and neutral cornering possible on the road, even when the Mercedes G is heavily loaded and has to pull heavy loads.

An SUV from Mercedes can hold up to 840 kg as its vehicle load capacity and pull up to an additional 2,800 kg, depending on the model and its features; under specially approved conditions, even up to 4,000 kg.

Initially, the G-Class was more part of the utility vehicle sector, which did not do justice to its extensive range of use as a recreational vehicle.

Below: With the introduction of the convertible top, handling when raising and lowering the top became a little easier.

After an extensive full restoration with long-term rust protection, this 280 GE chassis shows that it is fit for its continued life as a classic car. All W 460s are already entitled to the coveted H license plate number.

1986

Production of the panel van with a short wheelbase is discontinued. The G-Class has a new roof liner, a new dashboard in gray, and new seat covers with a big plaid pattern. Carpets, 16-inch aluminum rims, and seat heaters are available as new optional features. The standard equipment is supplemented by locking differentials, a rev counter, central locking, and a towing clutch at the front (these extras were previously available only for a surcharge). The G is now also available as a chassis with a cabin (wheelbase 2.85 m). Upon customer request, the 230 GE is also available with a catalytic converter.

Ausstattung Radio (Fabrikat Becker) auf Wuns

Toward the end of the production period for the W 460, the equipment became quite sophisticated, as here in the special "Classic" model.

1987

The chassis with cabin is now also available with a 3.12 m wheelbase. The 200 GE will first be produced. The convertible with a fold-down top replaces the covered car.

1988

The 250 GD replaces the 240 GD. A special series (200 units) of the 250 GD is sold with two-tone metallic paintwork. A double roller blind for the luggage compartment, an electric antenna, burl wood, armrests for the front seats, and electric windows complete the list of optional features. A new brake pad wear indicator and heated windshield washer jets are now part of the standard equipment.

1989

Plastic tanks are introduced for diesel vehicles. The special model of the 230 GE "Classic" (300 units) will be launched on the occasion of the tenth anniversary. Burl wood applications and a new ram guard are available as optional equipment.

1990

End of production of the 280 GE. The catalytic converter goes into series production on the 230 GE.

1991

The 300 GD is discontinued. In the W 460 series, only the 230 GE and 250 GD are available. Production of the W 460 series ended in August 1991.

41

For difficult axle articulation transitions, the locking differentials particularly prove their worth.

Small image: Until 1985, the seats had a fabric pattern in a small plaid, which was also used, by the way, in the 201 (190 E 2.3 16) and 124 model series. Then the design with the big plaid from the W 461 was adopted.

W 461

1993

The G model W 461 is available as the 230 GE and 290 GD. The versions of the body are identical to those of the W 460, while the convertible and short/open (civilian) versions are no longer available. The tanks now have a 96-liter capacity as standard. The well-known comfort extras from the W 460 series are done away with.

1994

Metallic paintwork is now also available on the W 461, and an additional version of the chassis is available (with 3.40 m wheelbase, 1.475 m track width, and 4,000 kg permissible gross vehicle weight).

1995

A double cabin for the 3.40 m chassis is presented but does not go into series production. Nevertheless, some double cabs are sold as custom-made units.

1996

The pickup version is discontinued.

1997

Production of the 230 GE is discontinued, and the 290 GD is replaced by the 290 GD Turbo. The W 461 gets new seats (from the W 463) and a new cockpit (from the Mercedes "Sprinter" van).

1998

ABS and airbags are available as options on the W 461.

1999

The W 461 will go into the next model year without any changes.

2000

The W 461 enters its last model year without any changes.

2001

Preliminary end of production of the W 461.

2002

Reintroduction of the W 461 for export markets. The G 270 CDI "Worker" is given the drivetrain from the W 463. The station wagon version is briefly discontinued.

At first glance, the cockpit of the W 461 differs from that of the W 460 due to the new steering wheel. The G-Class is particularly popular as a towing vehicle in difficult terrain.

The G 300 "Professional" is delivered with an air intake snorkel as standard equipment.

The W 461 in "wide version" with fender flares and 15-inch alloy wheels

43

The G 300 "Professional" is delivered with an air intake snorkel as standard equipment.

The civilian pickup version is one of the rarest G models.

Since 2003, the cockpit of the W 461 has been equipped with waterproof electronics (Worker, Pure, or Professional models).

The G 280/300 CDI, here in the "Pure" model from 2009. Since 2010, the vehicle has been available on the price list as the "Professional."

2004

In cooperation with Daimler AG, the Rheinmetall Landsysteme company develops two "Light Infantry Vehicles" based on the G 270 CDI: a universally operable vehicle with interchangeable modules in the rear (LIV), and a highly mobile reconnaissance and combat vehicle, the "AGF" (*Aufklärungs- und Gefechtsfahrzeug*: reconnaissance and combat vehicle) (LIV "Special Operations").

2005

The Canadian army buys 1,300 Mercedes G 270 GDI "Green Line" units as long station wagons. The vehicles will be equipped with, among other things, Michelin XCL MT tires in size 255/85/16, including a spare "tire donut" (which lets you keep driving when the tire goes flat), and special alloy wheels from Hutchinson. One group of the vehicles is armored; the others can be armored afterward, using a retrofit kit if necessary.

2006

No changes for the new model year.

2007

The 3-liter V6 CDI (G 280 CDI) engine replaces the 2.7-liter five-cylinder (G 270 CDI) in the "Green Line" or "Worker" models. The more powerful engine now also helps armored vehicles achieve satisfactory mileage.

2008

The "Green Line" is supplemented by a long chassis with three driven axles. The three-axle vehicle is one of the most amazing innovations in the G model; it was specially developed for army requirements. The Australian army orders 1,200 G 280 CDI, half of them as a three-axle vehicle.

2009

On the occasion of the thirtieth anniversary of production, the special G 280 CDI "Pure" model comes on the market. This car is based on the military version and can be had only as a long station wagon with a 24-volt electrical system. The production run, of 1,000 units, is quickly sold out.

Above: The cockpit of the W 461 has hardly changed over the course of the years.

The G 280 CDI "Pure," fully equipped with luggage rack, 7.5 J × 16-inch aluminum rims, and BF Goodrich AT tires

2010

Due to the success of the "Pure" version, Daimler will offer the G 300 CDI Professional starting in 2010. Unlike the "Pure," there is no limit set on the number of units. The Professional is available as a long station wagon, a long panel van, a chassis with driver's cabin, and a platform truck. Despite changes to the model designation, the technology remains unchanged except for the exhaust system.

G 300 CDI long panel van—again in the price list since 2010

A G 300 CDI
"Professional" with
6-inch steel rims as
standard equipment

The chassis with pallet,
with a gross vehicle
weight of up to 4,300 kg

Camping express: the Bimobil is a rather exclusive way to spend the night in your own car, far away from paved roads.

2011

The Australian army orders 1,200 Mercedes G 300 CDI Professionals, 400 of them as 6×6 models. The W 461 is presented with right-hand drive and becomes available in countries with left-hand traffic. The Bimobil company offers a recreational vehicle with the G 300 as a base.

2012

The Swedish army orders 400 Professionals, including some 6×6 models. All G 300 CDIs get passenger airbags as standard equipment. The Professional is given the steering wheel from the Mercedes Sprinter.

2013

The Swiss army orders 3,200 Professionals, including some vehicles as chassis with radio module. The G 300 CDI will not remain unscathed in the 2013 model update. The most-striking changes are the new passenger airbags and the newly redesigned dashboard with a useful tray in the middle. Far more important is the long-overdue reduction of load capacity with the normal spring rates on the rear axle. Now the vehicle is clearly able to travel significantly better, on- and off-road. To do this, the towing capacity is increased to 3.5 tons as standard, as on the other Gs. The model update is therefore a logical step toward a normal G for utility drivers.

2014

For the thirty-fifth anniversary of the start of production, Mercedes relaunches the China blue color on the Professional.

2015

Sales of the Professional are discontinued in the EU, due to strict exhaust gas regulations for diesel vehicles.

In 2012, the G 300 Professional was given an intake snorkel as standard equipment.

In Abu Dhabi, a G 300 CDI 6×6 for police and border guards will go on display at the IDEX arms trade fair.

2016

The W 461 goes into the new model year unchanged. A Light Armored Patrol Vehicle (LAPV) based on the G 300 CDI will be shown at the Eurosatory armaments fair in Paris.

2017

Daimler brings along a G 300 CDI 6×6 as an LAPV to IDEX in Abu Dhabi.

2018

The German Bundeswehr version of the LAPV Special Operations, developed on the basis of the W 461, will be shown at the Eurosatory in Paris.

2019

The W 461 goes into the new model year unchanged. It is built in the Graz plant on the same production line as the new W 463 A.

W 462

not being produced in Graz. These are the Peugeot P4, related to the G and built in France, as well as the Mercedes G, built in Greece for the Greek and Cypriot armies.

1982

Start of production of the Peugeot P4 for the French army. The French government calls for a "French automobile"; therefore, a suitable licensed product is sought. The Mercedes G/Peugeot vehicle concept prevails against their rivals, the VW Iltis/Citröen and Fiat Campagnola/ Renault. By the end of production in 1994, Peugeot had built 14,000 units of the P4; some 49 percent of the parts came from Mercedes (axles, transfer case, frame, body) and 51 percent from Peugeot (engine, transmission, doors, interior equipment). The spartan French version, with plastic doors and a low-power diesel engine, only hints at the qualities of the related G model. All Mercedes spare parts used in the P4 are listed internally under the spare-part numbers from the W 462.

The P4 VLTT (the official name) lacks almost all the comfort features of the civilian G. It is built as a 2.5-liter Peugeot diesel (model XD3 155) with a nominal output of 52 kW (70.5 hp). The top speed is 108 km/h. Between 1982 and 1992, some 15,000 P4s are built for the army and municipal purposes. The first 2,400 units are given a 2-liter gasoline engine with 79 hp at the Peugeot plant in Sochaux. The remaining vehicles are built in the former Panhard plant in Paris. The P4 is also deployed by the armies in Togo and Gabon.

1992

At the start of production in Greece, the G-Class is delivered as a CKD (completely knocked down)

version as individual parts and is assembled there. Technically, the vehicles correspond to the W 461 series. Production takes place in Thessaloniki at the ELBO (Hellenic Vehicle Industry S.A.) company (formerly Steyr-Hellas S.A.).

The first series, up to 1997, comprised 5,000 vehicles of the 240 GD model, which were delivered entirely as parts for assembly. The successor series comprised the 290 GD Turbo. Until 2001, the company produced open cars with a wheelbase of 240 cm, and chassis with pallet or trunk with a wheelbase of 312 cm.

2005

Panhard is developing a vehicle for the French army, special forces, on the basis of the G 270 CDI, which is similar to the German Bundeswehr's "Serval" model.

2017

Production of the G 300 CDI for the military and police begins in Algiers.

W 463

1990

Der W 463 startet als Station lang, Station kurz und Cabrio. Als Motoren werden der 230 GE, der 300 GE, der 250 GD und der 300 GD angeboten. Die Baureihe W 463 unterscheidet sich vor allem durch den permanenten Allradantrieb, der jetzt auch ABS-tauglich ist, und den luxusbetonten Innenraum vom W 460. Alle W 463 haben serienmäßig ein Fünf-gang-Schaltgetriebe. Ein Automatikgetriebe kann für die Varianten 300 GD, 230 GE und 300 GE optional geordert werden. Die Liste der Sonderausstattungen lässt keine Wünsche offen; so können erstmals im G Luxusextras wie Lederausstattung und elektrisches Schiebedach bestellt werden.

Heinrich Wangler, Mercedes test driver and known as "Mister G," drives the W 463 the way it should be driven. *Top left*: The Puch G 320 was the last G model sold as a Puch.

Top left: The Puch G 320 was the last G model sold as a Puch vehicle.

The cockpit of the 500 GE from 1993: there is a lot of burl wood and two-tone leather.

1991

The W 463 goes into the second model year unchanged. The secondary pump in the automatic transmission falls victim to the cost-controller's red pencil. From then on, it is no longer possible to tow anything with a G automatic. A development is started that keeps on taking things away from the G's off-road mobility.

1992

Introduction of the 350 GD Turbo. Burl wood, luggage compartment cover, cruise control (in combination with automatic transmission), stainless-steel running boards, and stainless-steel spare-wheel cover are available as optional extras.

1993

The 250 GD is discontinued and the 500 GE (M 117) is presented. The first V8 version of the G from Mercedes and Puch is available in a series of 500 units each. The car is produced only as a station wagon with amethyst-blue metallic paintwork.

1994

The 230 GE and 300 GD models are discontinued. ABS is now standard. AMG presents the 500 GE 6.0 AMG.

1995

The 320 GE replaces the 300 GE. Automatic transmission and wide axles (1.475 m) become standard

on all W 463s. For the new model year, the W 463 series is equipped with internally ventilated front disc brakes (from 500 GE), a driver airbag, an engine immobilizer, aluminum rims (7.5 × 16 inches), a side window aerial (except on the convertible), cruise control, a belt tensioner, a leather steering wheel, a tray in the center console, and bumpers in the body color for models with metallic paintwork. The antitheft alarm system is available as new optional equipment. The waterproof alternator with snorkel will be economized on; now, mud can get into the alternator. The retrofitting of the 300 GE alternator (with snorkel) is an option on some models.

1996

AMG introduces the G 36 and G 50 models. The G 300 turbo diesel replaces the 350 GD Turbo. All the G 300 TDs get the new electronically controlled, five-speed automatic transmission and front passenger airbags as standard. The G-Class was the world's first SUV with a five-speed automatic transmission. The convertible is the only SUV in the world to have an electrohydraulic soft top. The raised venting of the automatic transmission at the bulkhead under the hood is dispensed with. This is particularly problematic on long trips through deep water. However, the ventilation of the 300 GE can still be retrofitted.

1997

The G 320 (V6) replaces the 320 GE (R6). Air-conditioning, center armrests on the front seats, a

service interval display, and belt tensioners are part of the standard features. All W 463s are now delivered with the new five-speed automatic transmission.

1999

The G 500 (three-valve) is introduced. New optional extras such as tinted rear windows, Parktronic parking assistance, and 18-inch aluminum wheel rims are available on the G 500. All V8 models have chrome bars on the radiator grill, and stainless-steel door sills. The rear disc brake system is now standard equipment on all the W 463 series. To date, the M 113 is the only Mercedes engine that has made its market debut in the G-Class.

2000

The G 500 is available as a special-model "Classic" to mark the twentieth anniversary of production. The "Classic" series is limited to 400 units. The G 55 AMG is presented.

The multifunctional steering wheel is now standard on all W 463 models. The 2000 model year

enjoys cult status among fans. It is celebrated as the last of the almost electronics-free G-Class and still features such useful items as storage bins under the front seats and a second gearshift for the transfer case. The cars offer such comforts as a driver information system operated from the steering wheel, but without ESP, ETS, and the universal CAN bus system—and all that with up to 354 hp.

Although the W 463 in fact brings a little more weight to the terrain, it benefits from its basically open but lockable transfer case.

Left: The G 500 special series from the year 2000 was extremely lavishly outfitted.

From the W 463 to 2006, the second gearshift is no longer required (gear reduction is activated at the push of a button). The COMAND system is included as standard equipment on all V8 models within the scope of delivery.

2001

The G 400 CDI replaces the G 300 Turbo. The GPS "COMAND" navigation system is offered as optional equipment (with a TV tuner on request) in the G-Class (on the G 500 and G 400 CDI, it is standard). The second gearshift is no longer required; the reduction gear is now switched on electrically at the push of a button. A new heating and air-conditioning system replaces the old one, a rain sensor operates the windshield wipers as needed, a light sensor takes care of the headlights, and the fittings from the new C-Class are integrated into the completely redesigned G-Class interior, while the battery is moved to the center of the body. Beyond all this, a steering wheel that can be electrically adjusted in four directions is installed in the G as standard equipment.

2002

The G-Class is officially exported to the United States for the first time starting with the 2002 model year. The G 270 CDI is presented at the IAA in Frankfurt, and AMG presents the Pullman version of the G 55. The ESP stability program is now installed as standard, just as the BAS brake assistant is; the new 4-ETS traction control system adopted from the M-Class ensures proper traction on the road.

2003

As the models are changed, the G-Wagens are fitted with indicators integrated into the wing mirrors, and a new sound system from Harman Kardon is made available as an optional feature. The G 55 AMG is fitted with new 8.5-by-18-inch light-alloy wheels with 285/55 R 18 tires, larger fender flares, and a new exhaust system.

2004

AMG presents the G 55 AMG supercharger. On the occasion of the twenty-fifth anniversary of production, Mercedes launches a new "Classic" series. The G 55 AMG with naturally aspirated engine is dispensed with. In the rear seat, a three-point belt replaces the center lap belt, and a "window airbag" is available as an option.

2005

The G-Class continues unchanged into the 2005 model year.

2006

The engine software on the G 55 AMG is optimized; the top model now has 500 hp instead of 476.

Complete range: the G-Class, from 2001 to 2006, as presented entirely in silver as a convertible, short station wagon, and long station wagon

From 2007 to 2012, the W 463 had this beautiful cockpit with two classic round instruments.

2007

tarting in September 2006, the G 320 CDI will replace the G 270 CDI and G 400 CDI models and is currently the only diesel engine in the W 463. All G models are given xenon headlights and cornering lights in the new, now-oval-shaped fog lights.

Starting in April 2007, the model update will be implemented in full, with new taillights in LED design, new fittings, and the seven-speed automatic transmission on the G 500. The G 55 AMG sports exhaust system is available as an option on the G 500.

2008

The G-Class continues unchanged into the 2008 model year.

2009

For the model change into 2009, the G-Class is given a new grill with a three-louver design. The G 55 AMG radiator grill also features chrome inlays to mark its status as the top model. Besides this, the G 55 is given new wheel rims measuring 9.5 × 19 inches, and tires in the 275/50 R 19 size. The supercharged engine experiences an injection of power and from now on features 507 hp.

The G's audio, navigation, and multimedia system is given an extensive update.

In the long station wagon, the back-seat passengers can enjoy new back-seat lighting with integrated reading lights.

The most important innovation involves the G 500: the 5-liter, three-valve V8 (M 113), which has been installed since 1998, will now be replaced by the new 5.5-liter, four-valve V8 (M 273). The 388 hp unit offers a significant power boost of 90 hp compared to the M 113. The increase in torque is also noticeable; the G 500 now has a tremendous 530 newton meters (N m).

Starting from the 2009 model year, the G 500 can also be recognized by its aluminum wheel rims in the new double-spoke design. The tire pressure monitor is now also available as an option on the short-wheelbase models.

To mark the thirtieth anniversary, a special model of the G 500 long appears.

2010

The G 320 CDI is renamed as the G 350 CDI. A special series of the G 55 AMG supercharger, limited to just seventy-nine units, is presented in Dubai and delivered starting in 2010. The G 350 CDI Bluetec is presented in Geneva and, thanks to the AdBlue additive, meets the Euro 5 environmental standard.

55

Water features: the G 63 AMG right-hand drive wades through a stream on 20-inch tires.

Monitor: starting in 2012, the new COMAND system will have a freestanding screen.

2011

The G-model continues into the new model year unchanged.

2012

In the spring, the new G 63 is given V8 turbo engines. To do this, all systems are brought up to the latest standards of the other Mercedes model series. The G 65 with V12 engines from AMG is also presented. The short, closed G model is discontinued at the end of the 2012 model year (in August). A special model, called the "Last Edition," adopts the so-called BA3 construction design ("Bauausführung 3").

The G 55 AMG supercharger is discontinued. All G models now feature the seven-speed automatic. The vehicle interior is given a completely luxurious new design. Because of its large radiator, the G 63 has a new front bumper made of GRP, and a thinner underride guard made of aluminum. This impairs off-road mobility. With its 5.5-liter biturbo, the G 63 has 544 hp; the G 65, with its powerful 6-liter V12 biturbo, has 612 hp.

2013

In the G 63 AMG 6×6, Mercedes presents the "Über-G," which no one had thought possible. It has practically everything: both the AMG drivetrain from the W 463 and the 6×6 chassis and the portal axles from the military G 300 CDI model. The G 63 AMG 6×6 is conceptualized as a pure "fun car." A total of 170 units were sold.

2014

The G 500 Cabrio convertible appears in the "Last Edition 200." After that, with the convertible, the last short W 463 is also discontinued. AMG G 63 and G 65 are given the performance steering wheel. Updates are made to the command system.

At left, the G 500 Cabrio convertible from 2014 making its tame way along a country dirt road; *at right*, a G 63 AMG 6×6 from 2013 plows dramatically through the desert sand.

2015

The G 500 is given the 4-liter V8 biturbo M 176, with 422 hp, and a GRP front bumper with a larger radiator. The G 500 4×4 Squared is presented—a long station wagon with portal axles and 37-inch wheels. The remaining G models get power injection, while the G 63 AMG now delivers 571 hp, and the G 65 AMG has 630 hp and the G 350 CDI/Bluetec 245. The diesel now also is given the GRP bumper with large radiator.

2016

The W 463 goes into the 2016 model year unchanged.

2017

Mercedes presents the G 350d Professional, based on W 463 and the G 650 Maybach Landaulet, which was limited to ninety-nine units. The representation convertible with 6-liter V12 biturbo and portal axles is immediately sold out.

2018

The G 350d Professional and the G 500 4×4 Squared will be discontinued as the first W 463. Already by November, the G 500 and G 63 AMG are as good as sold out, since production will be switched to the new W 463 A in the second quarter of 2018. The last W 463s are delivered in the summer.

Everything at once, please: the G 650 Maybach Landaulet is extralong with a 6-liter V12 and portal axles.

The G 500 4×4 Squared has 12 cm more ground clearance and space for portal axles, thanks to its 37-inch wheels. The yellow fluorescent paint adds another 15,000 euros to the price tag.

W 463 A

The G 63 AMG (W 463 A) features front impact protection in its version with bumper bars. There is also a ram guard for the upper part of the front.

The specter that production of the G-Class will be shut down has been haunting the media since the late 1990s. The first M-Class had already been treated as the successor to the G model, and then the first GL-Class was treated as such. In reality, none of these vehicles could replace a G-Wagen, and it was selling better and better. With a recent success in sales, amounting to over 20,000 vehicles a year, there was likely to be enough money available to develop a successor. After thirty-nine years, a completely new development process was carried out for the first time. The W 463 A has exactly three carryover parts from its predecessor: the spare-wheel cover, the wiper and washer jets, and the door handles. Despite this, it was still supposed to look like

its predecessor, and a layperson would hardly notice any difference. However, apart from the ladder frame concept with rigid rear axles, everything is new. There is independent wheel suspension in the front, and the GLE, GLS, and X 350d models also have the transfer case—with chain belts instead of solid gear wheels. The back seat and dashboard also come from GLE/GLS.

The W 463 A is 11 cm wider, 8 cm longer, and 2 cm taller than its predecessor. Inside, it has become only 3 cm wider; the rear passengers have more space, and the cargo space has shrunk and is no longer level when the rear seat is folded down.

The driving dynamics on the road and the comfort level are worlds better than those of its predecessor. The

463 A is no longer a "workhorse." Instead, it has three locking differentials and massive suspensions, and despite its handicaps in detail, it is still an SUV.

2018

In January 2018, the W 463 A is presented to the public for the first time at the Detroit Auto Show. The G 500, with its 422 hp, 4-liter biturbo V8 (M 176), known from the W 463 model, will be the first to be showcased. The new G 63 AMG (M 177) likewise makes its debut in March with the V8. Both have nine-speed automatic transmissions.

2019

The G 350d is presented. It has a completely new 3-liter, in-line, six-cylinder biturbo with 286 hp, as well as the nine-speed automatic transmission.

2020

Added was an AMG version with the V8 M 177 and plug-in hybrid technology, as well as a new 4×4 Squared with portal axles and a more powerful G 400d diesel engine.

G 500 W 463 A: details such as the attached front turn signals have been retained. The headlights have "angel eyes" daytime running lights, and the interior is pure luxury.

The steel skeleton: All other body parts of the W 463 A are made of aluminum or plastic.

Right: The basis: the solid steel ladder frame of the W 463 A accommodates the drivetrain with independent suspension and the transfer case from the GLE models.

3. Versatility: Engines and Superstructures

"The hot V": The new V8 generation can be found in the G-Class as the M 176 (G 500) and M 177 (G 63 AMG). These 4-liter engines have two turbochargers.

64

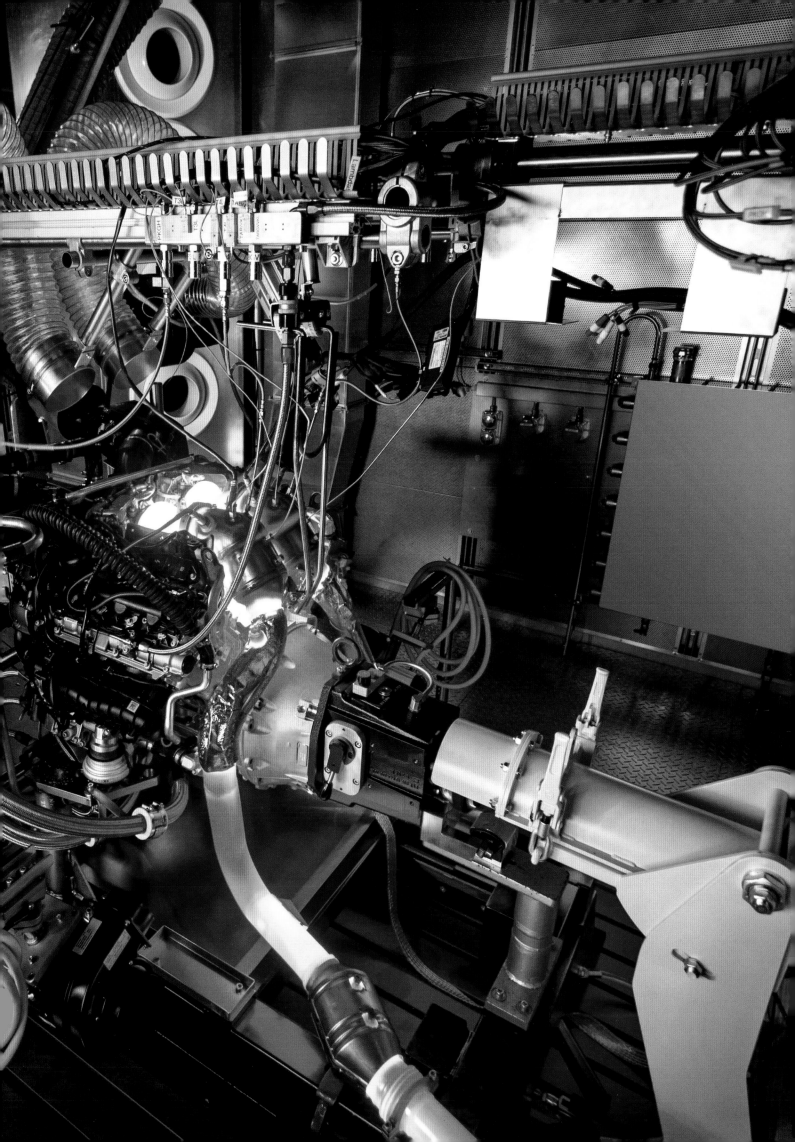

All Engines in Detail by Engine Displacement

200 GE (M 102 E 20)

The 2-liter engine with 118 hp, which originated from the W-124 limousine, was available only in Italy from 1987 onward; in that country, vehicles with engines of less than 2 liters cubic capacity were given tax breaks. The engine is largely identical in construction to the 230 GE.

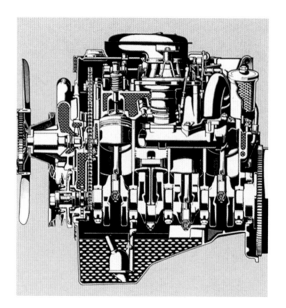

The M 115 from the 230 G with 90 or 102 hp

230 G (M 115)

In the beginning was the 230 G. The first series of open station wagon was available only with the 2.3-liter M 115 with 90 or 102 hp. It is the G-Wagen's "primeval engine." Almost all prototypes were equipped with it. Initially, Daimler and Puch had assumed that open cars would be the most-popular models. Then it was the long station wagon.

The weakest gasoline engine in the G-Class goes back to the power unit for the Mercedes 190 SL, made in 1955. This low-maintenance carburetor engine made its debut in 1973, with a displacement of 2.3 liters, in the Mercedes W 115 limousine. There are two versions in the G model, one with 90 hp (compression 8.1:1 for normal gasoline) and one with 102 hp (compression 9.0:1 for super gasoline).

The engine, which was equipped with a Stromberg 175 CD oblique-flow carburetor, always needs high revs to move the G and is correspondingly thirsty. Nevertheless, the 230 G can claim plenty of advantages; they are the lightest and technically least complicated G models. An open 230 G weighs a mere 1,740 kg, and almost every blacksmith in Africa can repair its carburetor engine. This model was built from 1979 to 1982.

The OM 616 from the 240 GD is the basic "bread-and-butter" diesel with 72 hp.

230 GE (M 102 E23)

The new 2.3-liter engine had an injection system from Bosch (KE-Jetronic). The power unit was part of the new generation of engines at Mercedes-Benz; in contrast to the old engines, which were sealed with a wear-prone Borgmann ring, these have a Simmer ring (radial shaft seal ring) to seal the crankshaft. The starter is located on the left side on the 230 GE (as well as on the 250 GD), which is why the transmissions that are used here are different from those in the other W 460 models. The four-cylinder engine was given its premiere in the Mercedes W 123 in 1981. In the W 460, the 125 hp (122 hp with catalytic converter) engine in the G model was considered a good compromise between the less powerful diesel engines and the fuel-efficient 280 GE. In the W 463, however, it was not very successful and was discontinued in 1994 after a short production period. Starting in 1986, a Bosch KE-Jetronic catalytic converter and hydraulic valve lifers were installed in this engine. The 230 GE was manufactured in the period from 1982 to 1996.

240 GD (OM 616)

The 2.4-liter, four-cylinder diesel made its debut in the Mercedes W 115, and the version installed in the G came from the W 123 series. It is supplied with diesel via a four-stamp pump from Bosch. The 72 hp of this basic "bread and butter" diesel with a 21:1 compression ratio is not ideal for the G-Class in

every respect. The "short" 5.33 axles nevertheless still make amazing climbing achievements possible when traveling off-road. The 240 GD was manufactured from 1979 to 1987.

250 GD (OM 602 D 25)

The five-cylinder engine was just like the 230 GE engine of the new generation, with the crankshaft

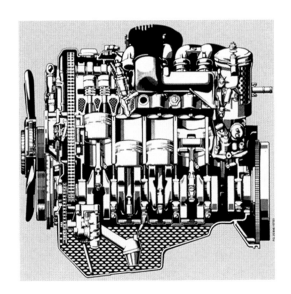

sealed by a Simmer ring and the starter on the left side. A five-stamp, in-line injection pump from Bosch took over supplying the engine's fuel. The economical machine, taken over from the W-124 sedan with its 84 hp, gives a convincing performance, especially off-road. The 22:1 compression ratio of the engine is not ideal for road traffic. The standard five-speed transmission and the ultrashort 6.17 (later 5.3) axles are the highlights of the 250 GD, which remained in the model range from 1987 to 1993.

G 270 CDI (OM 647)

The five-cylinder turbo diesel with 156 hp and 400 N m torque seems to be the perfect compromise between economy and power for the G. The engine, also familiar from the C- and E-Classes, has a so-called VNT (variable-nozzle turbine) turbocharger, with guide blades that can be adjusted according to the load condition of the engine. This allows the turbocharger to use the largest possible exhaust gas volume for compression of the intake air. This modern technology makes itself felt above all at low engine speeds by the rapid "response" of the turbocharger, as well as by means of better cylinder filling and the resulting higher torque. The first G 270 CDI came on the market in 2002. The same power unit also drives the W 461 "Worker," which has been back in production since 2003. The 270 CDI was replaced in 2006 by the 3-liter V6 CDI engine (G 280/300/320/350 CDI).

280 GE (M 110 E)

The Mercedes G, if properly motorized, can develop a dynamic that no one thought it was capable of. The 280 GE was the first G to demonstrate sports-car-like performance. The low-compression engine (8.0:1) runs on normal gasoline and is indestructible.

The engine can often survive even low oil and high temperatures (such as due to a defective radiator) without complaining. The legendary six-cylinder, double-camshaft engine with Bosch K-Jetronic was launched in 1972 in the Mercedes 280 SE (W 116). It is exceptionally robust and turns at up to 6,500 rpm; its performance (156 hp) enables it to reach a top speed of 155 to 165 km/h (depending on the gear ratio). The engine reaches its maximum torque (226 N m) only at 3,200 rpm. Despite this, the 280 GE performs incredibly when traveling off-road but is also a well-powered, comfortable, and fast touring car. The M 110 has a cast-iron engine block and a crankshaft with seven bearings. The engine superstructure, including oil pan, cylinder block, cylinder head, camshaft box, and valve cover, requires a large number of seals.

The passenger car version of the M 11 has pistons with a "hump" that, together with the cylinder head design, form a hemispherical combustion chamber. If you replace the low-compression G engine (with flat pistons) with an M 110 E from a corresponding Mercedes passenger car series, the G-Wagen's performance increases to around 170 hp. This was done on some vehicles for the Dakar Rally. The G oil pan must be used in the converted vehicle, however, because of the baffle plates and the necessary clearance

for the front axle, and the G intake manifold must also be used, for space reasons. The only drawback to the 280 GE is its fuel consumption—the high-revving engine consumes around 20 liters of standard gasoline. The car compensates its drivers for this with an engine sound that is almost addictive. The sonorous sound of the six-cylinder engine is simply unsurpassed. Starting in 1985, the 280 GE's performance dropped to 150 hp due to stricter exhaust regulations. The 280 GE was manufactured for ten years, from 1979 to 1990.

280 GE AMG (M 110 E)

It wasn't possible to increase the engine displacement in the 280 GE because the engine had already reached its

Right: The OM 602 from the 250 GD powers the original Bundeswehr "Wolves" at 84 hp.

Left: The DOHC six-cylinder M 110 model from the 280 GE, with 156 hp, always run reliably even under extreme conditions.

67

maximum potential when it came from the factory. The engine block went back to the 220 SE engine from the 1960s. Expansion to 2.8-liter displacement left no room for tuning the cylinders. AMG achieved a performance of 220 hp with conventional cylinder head machining and sports car camshafts. The AMG engine revs at over 7,000 rpm and enhances all the strengths of the 280 GE. Happy are those G drivers who now call one of these rare engines their own.

290 GD (OM 602 D 29)

The five-cylinder diesel engine from the Mercedes commercial vehicle series 210 D to 410 D, which is installed only in the W 461, is robust and reliable, but with 95 hp it is not the most powerful engine for the G-Class. The unit has a compression ratio of 22:1 and is supplied by a five-cylinder, in-line injection pump from Bosch. The 290 GD was produced between 1992 and 1996.

290 GD Turbo (OM 602 DLA 29)

The five-cylinder TDI engine with intercooler from the Mercedes "Sprinter" van is not only reliable and robust, but with 120 hp it is also powerful enough to keep a heavy G-Class moving. In addition, at around 11.5 liters per 100 km, fuel consumption is very reasonable for a G model. The electronics required for the injection system are kept to a minimal level. The 290 GDT was equipped with the four-speed automatic

transmission from the W 463 and rear disc brakes as standard features. Besides this, a new front axle housing was also used to accommodate the gear pairing for the extremely long axle ratio (3.95:1). The 290 GD Turbo production period lasted from 1997 to 2001.

280 CDI/300 CDI (OM 642)

The 3-liter V6 CDI engine in the "280" development stage is reserved for the "Green Line" models. The unit represents a significant improvement compared to its predecessor (270 CDI), primarily in terms of performance and smoothness, and it moreover consumes barely more than the five-cylinder did. The temperament of the V6, with 184 hp at 3,800/min. and 540 N m from 1,600/min. to 2,400/min., now also appears to be appropriate for professional driving. The standard five-speed automatic transmission is very robust and low maintenance; it fits perfectly with the G 280 CDI. The armored military versions, weighing up to 4.5 tons, had suffered much more with the "old" 270 CDI, due to the extremely weak V6.

300 GE (M 103)

The 300 GE took over as the heavy successor of the 280 GE in 1990. Although it does in fact generate more power (170 hp) than the 280, it does this at a higher engine speed level. Despite all the technical and comfort-related advantages of the W 463, and its considerably higher top speed, in fact everyone missed

also with its great reliability, especially compared with other well-tuned M 103 engines. In 1988, the engine conversion cost 17,000 deutsch marks (DM) at AMG, including value-added tax.

The M 103 impresses with its smooth running and easy maintenance.

300 GD (W 460) (OM 617)

The diesel engine in the G model comes from the W-123 sedan. However, the reliable five-cylinder diesel engine (OM 617) had already celebrated its debut in 1974 in the W 115.

The 88 hp engine is basically identical to the 240 GD—it has just one more cylinder. In particular, the combination of this motorization with the "long" five-speed gearbox and the small tires (235/70-15

the 280 GE and, above all, its unique sound. However, the 300, which comes from the W 124, is 41 kilograms lighter than the 280 GE's engine due to numerous weight-optimized light-alloy parts (cylinder head, pistons, oil pan, etc.) but also has only one overhead camshaft (two shafts in the 280 GE). The M 103 was a fundamentally new design, with many parts identical to the OM 601/602/603 diesel engines and the M 102 four-cylinder gasoline engine. The specific fuel consumption and maintenance requirements were lower than for the M 110.

The M 103 had an engine block made of gray cast iron and a cross-flow cylinder head made of aluminum, with two V-shaped valves per cylinder. These were operated by a centrally located, chain-driven camshaft, via rocker arms with hydraulic valve clearance compensation. The M 103 was equipped with Bosch KE–Jetronic fuel injection and an electronic ignition system, with a matching connector in the engine compartment to adjust the ignition timing to different qualities of fuel. The unit's smooth running is first class; the M 103 is one of the quietest six-cylinder engines ever built. The 300 GE, which like all W 463s has a regulated catalytic converter, was produced from 1990 to 1994.

The OM 617 was the most powerful standard diesel in the G-Class.

or 225/75 R16) has proven itself in practice. The production period for the 300 GD (W 460) lasted from 1979 to 1990.

300 GD (W 463) (OM 603)

The 300 GD (W 463) has taken over only the name from its predecessor; otherwise it is worlds apart from the 300 GD in the W 460 series. The silky-smooth 113 hp, six-cylinder engine, taken from the W 124 series, is

G 32 AMG (M 103 E32)

On the basis of the M 103, AMG developed a 3.2-liter version with 240 hp at 5,750 rpm. The G models with this engine are extremely rare. Due to the higher torque of 320 N m at 4,500 rpm, a G with this engine appears to be much more potent.

Until the market launch of the 500 GE in 1993, the AMG M 103 represented one of the few affordable options for enhancing the performance of the 300 GE that was suitable for everyday use and affordable. AMG sold more than 500 of the M 103 3.2—but mostly in W 124 (300 E) or W 201 (190 E) models. The engine made an impression not only with its performance, but

The OM 603 provides an always reliable 113 hp.

69

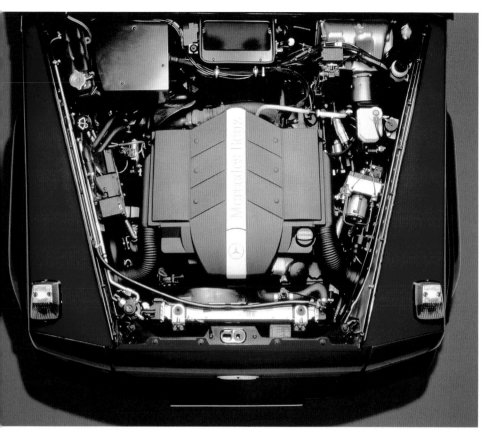

Top right: The G 300
Turbo diesel with its 177
hp is really lively on the
road.

already an enormous step forward by itself compared to the five-cylinder model in the W 460. The modern engine with light-alloy cylinder head has new diesel preheating and a compression ratio of 22:1. The 300 GD (W 463) rolled off the production lines from 1990 to 1994.

G 300 Turbo Diesel (OM 606 LA)

The G 300 turbo diesel opened up completely new performance perspectives for the G model. Due to the fact that an intercooler is now installed in the factory, the G 300 turbo diesel no longer has any thermal problems, in comparison to the 350 Turbo. In addition, the diesel generator set was equipped with control

The V6 engines of the G 320 shine in their smooth running and exemplary exhaust emissions.

electronics that prevent the engine from overheating through automatic throttling. The four-valve motor comes from the W 140 (S-Class). The G 300 TD was the fastest diesel SUV of its time and rounds off the G range between 1996 and 2001.

G 320 CDI / G 350 CDI (OM 642)

The 3-liter V6 CDI engine in the "320" development stage combines the best features of its two predecessors (270 CDI and 400 CDI). It does not consume much more fuel than the five-cylinder (270 CDI) and almost approaches the temperament of the V8 (400 CDI). With 224 hp at 3,800 rpm and 540 N m from 1,600 to 2,400 rpm, the V6 moves the G along at a very lively pace. Thanks to the standard seven-speed automatic transmission, the G 320 CDI shines with superior acceleration (8.5 seconds from 0 to 100 km/h) and a top speed (185 km/h). At the beginning of the series, however, there were software problems with the automatic system, which sometimes led to wild switching maneuvers. An exchange of the software brought improvement here. Starting in mid-2010, the 350 CDI would also be available as an environmentally friendly "Bluetec." It had only 211 hp, and then 245 starting in 2014.

320 GE (M 104 E32)

This 3.2-liter, six-cylinder machine is a real stroke of luck. The unit, designed for super gasoline, with four valves per cylinder and two overhead camshafts, has the pithy sound of the 280 GE and is just as free revving, but no longer as engine speed dependent as the 300 GE. The 210 hp and especially the 300 N m torque are at the vehicle's disposal much sooner than on the 300 GE, which of course makes off-road driving much easier. A disadvantage of the 320 GE is that the motor takes in air in the direction of travel, which increases the risk of a water hammer. The 320 GE—in the range from 1994 to 1998—had a standard four-speed automatic transmission and long transfer case from the 350 GD. The model's Achilles' heel is its corrosion-prone ignition cable.

G 36 AMG (M 104 E 36)

The 272 hp high-revving engine is a real alternative to the V8. It reinforces all the advantages of the 320. In terms of performance, it almost reaches the level of the 5.6-liter V8. Due to the series production of the C 36 AMG, the M 104 E 36 engines are comparatively readily available. Engines from appropriate "parts-donor" vehicles are ideal for retrofit installation in the G 320. Important: When making a conversion, the engine control unit must also be adapted!

G 320 (V6, M 112)

The three-valve V6 engines with dual ignition made their entry into the G-Class in 1998. The V6, with a 90° included angle between cylinder rows, consumes less fuel than the old 320 and has particularly good emission values. Thanks to a balance shaft, the environmentally friendly unit runs with low vibrations and is also acoustically more restrained compared to the 320 GE (R6). In terms of weight, the V6 sets new standards with sophisticated lightweight-construction technology, including cylinder tracks made of a silicon-aluminum alloy and structures of aluminum and magnesium die castings. In addition, a switchable intake module provides an increase in torque in the lower speed range; from 2,800 rpm, the maximum 300 N m is available. In terms of power output, however, the 215 hp engine is superior to the in-line six-cylinder only on paper; their differences are marginal in practice. The most significant step forward in the G 320 is the perfect, electronically controlled, five-speed automatic transmission. The V6 engine was in the model range from 1998 to 2001.

350 GD Turbo (OM 603 D 35A)

It took thirteen years for a turbo-diesel engine to make its debut in the G-Class. The power unit from the W-140 sedan (S-Class) delivered a decent torque to the SUV for the first time. But the engine of the 350 GD

The Brabus 350 GD Turbo can be recognized by the intercooler under the front bumper.

The engine of the G 400 CDI is potent, but also complex. Anyone who is traveling in Morocco or farther afield should really value meticulous maintenance.

The V8 diesel of the G 400 CDI

The in-line, six-cylinder engine delivers 286 hp and, with a maximum torque of 600 N m at 1,200 to 3,200 rpm, is more powerful than ever before. The engine fulfills the European 6d TEMP emissions standard with the help of AdBlue. The fill pipe opening is integrated into the vehicle's outside tank recess.

G 400 d (OM 656)

The engine of the G 400d, based on the 3-liter, in-line six-cylinder, is the more powerful version of the OM 656, with 340 hp and 700 N m torque. The G 400d made its debut in model year 2020.

G 400 CDI (OM 628)

The G 400 was a real revolution; no other diesel SUV in the world can shine with comparable torque on the axle, none have this degree of comfort, and none have an equivalent safety-and-traction package. The V8 turbo diesel is one of the most powerful passenger car diesels in the world; it suits the G-Class like no other engine. The 250 hp, two turbochargers, an intercooler, and four valves per cylinder all deliver a fantastically high torque of 560 N m from 1,700 rpm.

Like the G-Class itself, this motor brings together a collection of technical highlights: four-valve technology, common rail system, throttled-intake high-pressure pump, biturbo charging with variable-geometry turbo (VNT technology), water intercooling, exhaust gas recirculation, and electrically actuated intake air throttling, as well as lightweight cylinder heads and crankcases. The technical data of this sovereign engine are impressive. In addition, it operates much more economically compared to the G 500.

The G 400 CDI remained in the model range since December 2001 and was replaced in 2006 by the 3-liter V6 CDI engine (G 320/350 CDI). In a way similar to the 350 GD Turbo, the G 400 CDI initially struggled with many shortcomings (including timing-chain control), but these were gradually fixed.

When purchasing this model, it is a very good idea to have a well-supplied checkbook for maintenance expenses. The involved vehicles come from the 2001 to 2003 production years; starting in 2004, the 400 CDI became generally reliable. Conversion to the components from the series from 2004 onward is definitely possible. To do this, the control chain must be replaced and the cylinder heads must be overhauled as well, the fan bearings must be replaced, and the electronics must be updated to the standard for 2004. If you go to an experienced engine builder, this will set you back by around 7,000 euros. For this, you get an absolutely reliable V8 turbo diesel.

Turbo, with an automatic transmission as standard, is considered the most responsive G engine. The Garrett turbocharger produces 0.9-bar boost pressure and generates an enormous amount of heat, which is a big disadvantage for the cylinder head.

As standard, all 350 GD Turbos are equipped with an engine oil cooler, which is set in the right fender and gets its fresh air through a grill. The precautionary retrofitting of a charge air cooler or an additional engine oil cooler is highly recommended here. In the 350 GD Turbo's first two model years (1992 to 1993), thermally induced engine failures occurred often, but from the second generation (model year 1994) on, these were brought under control by installing a reengineered and much more stable version.

For the first time, the longer (0.87:1) transfer case was installed in the 350 GD Turbo. The 350 GD was manufactured from 1992 to 1996. If an engine is affected by the heat problems that occurred at the start of production (1992–1994), the following measures are necessary to achieve a permanent solution: replacement of the cylinder head with the last version (from 1995), replacement of the water pump with a larger one with a new large pulley, and replacement of the radiator with the version from 1995. Although all this is costly and time consuming, with these measures the last purely mechanical turbo-diesel engine in the G-Class comes close to achieving eternal life.

G 350d (OM 656)

The new OM 656 diesel engine will enter the new G-Class in 2019 with stepped combustion bowls, two-stage turbocharging, and variable valve control.

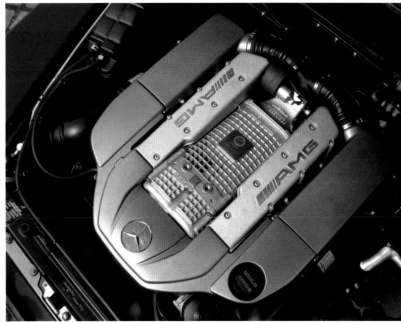

500 GE (M 117 E 50)

Customers had to be patient until 1993 before they could buy a G-Class with V8 engine directly from Mercedes-Benz. In cooperation with AMG (which had already retrofitted several 280 GEs and 300 GEs with V8 engines), Mercedes-Benz developed the potent 500 GE.

The first models were limited to a total of 1,000 vehicles, 500 each from Puch and Mercedes-Benz. The 500 GE vehicles, available exclusively as the long-model station wagon, were lavishly outfitted, but they were certainly not a special sale item. Mercedes demanded just under 180,000 DM (including value-added tax) for such a vehicle. Nevertheless, this special series sold out quickly.

The 240 hp, 5.0-liter aluminum engines (M 117) made their debut, just like the G-Class, in 1979 (then in the Mercedes 450 SLC 5.0 aluminum coupe). The current version of the 215 kg engine is powered by a Bosch KE–Jetronic and comes from the W 126 (S-Class).

In contrast to the newer four-valve engines (M 119), the two-valve engines fit into the narrow engine compartment in the G model. Its four-speed automatic transmission also comes from the 126 series. The 500 GE has more-powerful, ventilated disc brakes on the front axle, and the engine oil cooler from the 350 GD Turbo, including the exhaust grill in the right fender and the 0.8:1 transfer case. All 500 GEs were delivered without a locking differential on the front axle.

500 GE 6.0 AMG (M 117 E 60)

The 300 or 331 hp (without catalytic converter) strong V8 is proving to be a true powerhouse for the G-Class.

The AMG 6.0 was the first G to surpass the 200 km/h mark. The power unit from Affalterbach, Germany, was also installed in the emergency vehicles for Klaus Seppi and Clay Regazzoni, who competed in the 1989 Paris-Dakar Rally.

G 500 (M 113 E 50)

As soon as you get in it, the G 500 shows it is an exceptional vehicle, with the bluish-glowing "Mercedes-Benz" lettering in the door sills. After a nineteen-year production period, a G-model V8 with a good 300 hp of power finally went into series production. The G 500 was even the first Mercedes with the new narrow three-valve V8. For the first time, engine output corresponded to the other G-Class qualities.

The G 500 has enhanced the model range since 1998. The 5-liter V8, which is related to the V6, has a compression ratio of 10.1:1 and is equipped with dual ignition (two spark plugs per combustion chamber), but economy is not one of its virtues. An electronically controlled intake module increases the torque yield in the lower speed range and ensures that the engine can always spontaneously respond to the driver's demand for performance, in the city or on country roads.

The V8 accelerates the G with brute force, and never before has driving a G-Wagen been so much fun. Dunes that used to be considered insurmountable are suddenly no longer an obstacle, and on level ground this car moves forward at 199 km/h. At its debut, the G 500 became the most powerful SUV in the world and is capable of top performance especially when driving off-road—and unlike the 500 GE, it has a front-axle locking differential. The very well-equipped G 500

Left: The V8 of the G 500

The AMG supercharged V8: haute école of engine building

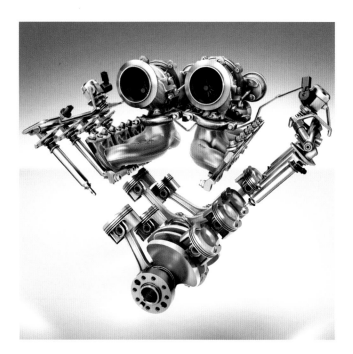

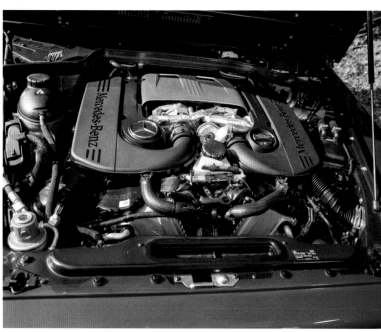

The two loaders are located between the cylinder banks on the M 178. Incidentally, the V8 is also at work in the 2019 Aston Martin Vantage.

Right: The new biturbo V8 first appeared in the AMG GT and replaced the M 273 naturally aspirated engine.

(leather, air-conditioning, burl wood, 18-inch wheels) costs about 10,000 DM more than a G 320, if you adjust for the cost of all the outfitting. Anyone who wanted to be a bit more classy on the road could order the G 500 Classic in 1999; this special model gleamed in its full range of elegant features.

G 500 (M 273) (in the United States: G 550)

Starting in September 2008, the G 500 has been equipped with the new 5.5-liter, four-valve V8 with 388 hp at 6,000 rpm. The M 273 is the more advanced version of the M 113. It took over the cylinder spacing and arrangement from the latter. The high-performance unit helps the G 500 achieve sprinter capabilities, with a powerful 530 N m torque at 2,800–4,800 rpm. Thus, the G 500 can accelerate from 0 to 100 km/h in just 5.9 seconds, and the top speed is curtailed to 210 km/h. At 17.4 liters per 100 km, fuel consumption is significantly lower than that of the G 500 with its predecessor M 113 power unit.

G 500 (M 176)

The new biturbo V8, with an engine displacement of just 4 liters, made its debut in the AMG GT sports car and replaced the 5.5-liter, naturally aspirated engine (M 273) in the G 500. The 422 hp power unit has advantages in terms of performance and fuel consumption. But these are dearly bought because of the large radiators, inconveniently located—because it puts them at risk—in the front bumper, which is now also made of vulnerable GRP. Worth noting: the turbochargers are housed in the V of the engine.

G 55 AMG (M 113)

Anyone who really wants to be able to drive at 215 km/h in a Mercedes G buys the G 55 AMG. The engine yanks this heavy car from standing still to traveling 100 km/h in 6.8 seconds. The G 55 creates an incredible spectacle on the highway as the vehicle it has just passed realizes that it is being outpaced by an SUV at 200 km/h. The 354 hp transforms the G into a sports car. When accelerating around curves, the inner front tire (without 4ETS) smokes as it spins. The chrome side pipes leave no doubt as to their sports car origins. The 5.5-liter V8 is available on eleven AMG models. It has a longer stroke, sharper camshafts, and a moderately increased compression ratio of 10.5:1. The engine, which comes with a factory warranty, has forged aluminum pistons that are cooled by specially developed oil spray nozzles. The torque of 525 N m is available at as low as 3,000 rpm. The unit is fueled by means of a microprocessor-controlled injection system. This engine, which purrs quietly in the S-Class, is transformed into a roaring sports car engine in the G-Class. At speeds of over 170 km/h, however, the V8 sound is suffocated by the roar of the airstream. The brakes deliver maximum power to slow down the heavy G-Wagen from over 200 km/h, but they handle the task with ease. This AMG model is the ultimate driving machine.

G 55 AMG supercharger (M 113)

The 476 hp in a G-Class provides for a powerful adrenaline rush. While the G 55 was already an incredible design, the supercharger is "an automobile from another star." With the introduction of the 450 hp Porsche Cayenne Turbo, it appears that the last taboo has been broken. Since the Porsche model was also selling extremely well then, Mercedes was forced to take action and continue the momentum. It was enough to combine the G 55 and the AMG supercharged engine. The G 55 supercharger is just as expensive as a Cayenne Turbo, but it accelerates faster, in the blink of an eye. The force of 700 N m catapults the G to 100 km/h in 5.6 seconds—the G, which can theoretically reach a speed of 240 km/h, is actually "closed off" at 210 km/h. The engine reaches 476 hp at 6,100 rpm; the torque of 700 N m, at between 2,650 and 4,500 rpm.

The V8 supercharged engine was honored as the "Best Performance Engine" at the International Engine Awards 2003 (the "Oscars" for engines). The G 55 K passes the magical mark of 200 km/h, which most G-Class cars never reach, after twenty-three seconds. Extensive modifications are necessary to install the engine. The drivetrain and chassis are modified as a result. An even more powerful braking system ensures proper deceleration, and as with all G-Class engines, a special oil pan is installed to guarantee a reliable supply of the lubricant to the engine when the vehicle is at a slant. A total of three intercoolers supply the supercharger with cool air, and a powerful electric intake fan sustains the engine's water cooler. With the G 55 supercharger, AMG is demonstrating the enormous potential that lies in the G-Class. As part of all this, the four-flow exhaust system emits a deep V8 sound.

G 55 supercharger with 500 hp (M 113)

With the market launch of the G 55 AMG supercharger with 476 hp (with 500 hp in the standard spurt from 0 to 100 km/h, or from 0 to 60 mph), Mercedes displaced the Porsche Cayenne Turbo from pole position. Porsche upped the ante with the 520 hp Cayenne Turbo S. In a spurt, it was a blink of an eye faster than the powerful 476 hp G 55 AMG supercharger. However, with the 500 hp G 55 supercharger, Mercedes is now correcting the ranking order again.

The G 55 is and remains the "King of SUVs." The fact that the G is able to accelerate faster despite having less power is due, on the one hand, to the slightly lower vehicle weight compared to the Cayenne Turbo, but above all, to the fact that the G has the more stable drivetrain. As a result, the AMG engine is able to unleash all its power and its mighty torque—even starting out from the lowest level of engine speed—on to the wheels without restraint. In the 2009 model year, the G 55 got another injection of power and has featured 507 hp since then.

The G 63 AMG with the M 278 in the partial load range is bewitching with its purring turbo.

G 63 AMG (M 278)

The new 5.5-liter biturbo V8 is based on the M 273, which is certainly well known from the G 500. It replaces the M 113 supercharger engine of the same size. The 544 hp power unit features a few advantages over the latter in terms of performance and fuel consumption but, above all, has the disadvantage of the exposed radiator in the fragile bumper. The G 63 came with the seven-speed automatic right from the start. The turbochargers are flanged to the outside of the cylinder banks.

G 63 AMG (M 176)

The 4-liter biturbo V8, familiar from the G 500, also replaces the 5.5-liter biturbo M 278 in the G 63 AMG. The 585 hp power unit develops almost incredible performance in conjunction with the new nine-speed automatic transmission.

G 65 (M 279), G 650 Maybach

Rumor has it that the only reason the G 65 AMG, with a 6-liter V12 biturbo, is on the price list at all is to the credit of the emir of Qatar. Until now, the V12 was available only from Brabus, as well as in a few unique items from AMG. But now the emir absolutely wanted a V12 G from Mercedes—no matter what it cost. The answer was as expected: "That just won't work. For this to be worth our while, we would already have to manufacture several vehicles." "All right then, how many?" "A hundred." "Then I'll order a hundred."

The V12 was available in the G 63 for a 100,000-euro surcharge, as well as with initially 612 and then 630 hp and a 230 km/h top speed. A production run of 300 units per year makes it one of the most exclusive G-Class vehicles—and it has one of the most stable values over time: a G 65 AMG certainly does not come cheap. The Last Edition—sixty-five vehicles at a unit price of 330,000 euros—was immediately sold out. The engine was also installed in the G 650 Maybach Landaulet.

77

The new star in the SUV heavens: the G 500 W 463 A

Superstructure Versatility in Detail

Plain, but beautiful: in the first generation, the W 463 convertible managed without any enhancements.

Open, short model with folding windshield, construction design (Bauausführung [BA] 7) (military version only, 1979 to date)

The military gets the G-Class in a special open model. With no roof rails, a removable rollover bar, and a fold-over windshield, this version offers ideal visibility for off-road driving.

Open, long model with folding windshield, construction design, BA 10 (military version only, 1981 to date)

This version, too, is preferentially manufactured for the armed forces of various countries. For this model, the same features apply as for the short military G, but up to ten people can ride in the long version.

Open, short, covered vehicle, BA 1
(1979 to 1991; starting in 1986, only the military version)

The roof of the covered vehicle is watertight and draft free, features that are anything but usual for SUVs. However, this component generates an enormous background noise even at slow speeds, and at high speeds the noise is deafening. It takes about ten minutes for two people to take the top down; the roof rails are screwed together and are best left in place. Meanwhile, there are "bikini" and compact tops for this model available from the car accessory trade.

The Landaulet model, which is probably the only one of its kind in the world capable of off-road driving, offers airy, luxurious seats.

Open, long, covered vehicle
(military version only, 1981 to date)

This model is manufactured almost exclusively to fulfill military orders. The long covered vehicle can also carry up to ten people.

Open, short, convertible top (1985 to 1996)

The covered vehicle was not for pampered Mercedes customers; this was also recognized in Stuttgart, and the convertible top provided a remedy. The convertible top, which can survive wind, weather, and the car wash, is much easier to open up than the canvas top. Above all, the roof frame was gone when driving with the top down. The noise from the wind with the new fabric roof was also significantly less than with the earlier covered car. The convertible was at the same time a five-seater station wagon with plenty of storage space, and that on a vehicle that takes up a road area of only 4.27 m. The top cover is like the one on the 107 series (SL).

Convertible top, long, automatic

The Baur bodywork company in Stuttgart built four-door convertibles that were based on the extralong

G-Class. The extremely expensive and very rare vehicles were destined for export markets without exception. This vehicle was presented in a modified design as the G 650 Maybach special series. The portal-axle vehicle, which was limited to ninety-nine units, has a closed compartment for the driver and an open, extremely luxurious rear space.

Convertible top, automatic, BA 1 (1996 to today)

An electrohydraulic convertible top on an SUV—only on the Mercedes G! The shape of the G convertible is rather unusual, with its triangular windows on the B pillar. The three-layer top seriously reduces the wind noise; it is raised and lowered using two hydraulic cylinders. The locking mechanism comes from the locks on the W 124 Cabriolet. The flutter-free soft top opens within thirty seconds of activating the opening mechanism. A wind deflector is available for convertible drivers who are sensitive to drafts.

Short station wagon, BA 2 (1979 to today)

The three-door G, in its highly maneuverable, short station wagon model, works particularly well for singles. With its compact dimensions (length, 4.11 to 4.23 m), it is comparable to a VW Golf II but still offers plenty of space for passengers and luggage. The short wheelbase gives you clear advantages when driving off-road, and its small turning circle is a big help when maneuvering with a trailer hitched on. However, without special approval, the allowable trailer load is lower than that for the long station wagon.

Long station wagon, BA 6 (1979 to today)

The spacious long station wagon is the bestselling version of the G-Wagen. In the five-door version, it is the perfect family and touring car, and this version also has the biggest trailer-towing capacity of all the G models. Depending on the model and legal regulations, up to ten people can ride in the long station wagon. Just

Above: The W 463 convertible is the only SUV with an electric soft top.

For popes and just-married couples—the G 500 Landaulet from the specialist car body maker Baur

81

Above: Indomitable: the W 461 as station wagon / short (*above*) and the long version (*right*)

Below: Long open G military model; here, a restored 2009 vehicle

Only a very few G models with double cabins were manufactured as pickups; this one was rebuilt using original Mercedes parts.

like the short station wagon, the long model offers an amazing amount of space for passengers and luggage for the very small amount of road space it occupies (4.58 to 4.68 m). It is therefore shorter than a Mercedes W 124 (E-Class).

Extralong station wagon (2002 to 2017)

The AMG Pullman model is built using two G-Class bodies; a long and a short body are combined on a super-long frame to construct a Pullman car body. The XXL-G seems to be particularly appropriate for sheiks with a lot of followers or for pop and film stars.

Short panel van, BA 2 (1981 to 1986)

The short van didn't stay in the official Mercedes-Benz program for very long. When a G model was ordered as a transport vehicle, then it was usually the long version with more loading capacity.

Above: This 6×6 with double cabin is a test vehicle for the Australian army order.

Left: This converted Bundeswehr Wolf has tarpaulin doors and the matching trailer.

Long panel van, BA 4 (1981 to 2002)

The long panel van also wasn't a real sales success, but an interesting alternative was expanding it to make a vehicle for long trips.

Pickup, BA 5 (1985 to 1996)

With its lengthwise side seats and windows, up to ten people could travel in a panel van. The pickup is a real rarity, which may be due to the fact that pickup vehicles in general aren't very common in Europe. In addition, the high price of this model certainly didn't promote sales.

The G in the Pullman model
_____

Chassis with driver's cabin (2.85 m), BA 9 (1986 to 1992)
People often consider the chassis as a base for carrying a recreational-vehicle superstructure, but actually the biggest customer for these is the military. The chassis is delivered to them with a paramedic supply truck body built on as a superstructure.

Chassis with driver's cabin (3.12 m), BA 9 (1987 to 1994)
To create more space for carrying a superstructure, Mercedes also built the chassis with a longer wheelbase.

Chassis with driver's cabin (3.40 m), BA 9 (1994 to 2001)
This very big chassis is not only longer, it also has a bigger overall width of 1.84 m due to wider tracking (1.550 m).

Chassis with driver's cabin (3.40 m, 4.4 tons) (2009 to today)
The 4.6-ton chassis can be recognized by its stronger axles, stronger springs, and 17.5-inch tires. This vehicle is primarily made for the range of partially armored military models.

Chassis with driver's cabin (3.40 m), BA 11 double cabin (1994 to 2001)
This huge vehicle, which was built exclusively on special order, is used mostly as a workshop wagon. The "double cabin" was manufactured as the 290 GD and 290 GD Turbo. The last DoKa (for *Doppelkabine*, "double cabin") model, with a 120 hp turbo-diesel engine, is an especially sought-after vehicle today. It represents the top of the G-Class in the utility vehicle sector. These are very spacious vehicles with almost unlimited use potential. As so often in the history of the G-Class, the high price was a reason for the small number of DoKa vehicles. Most of these vehicles were sold as Puch models.

Full-size diesel pickup
Daimler AG offers this four-door double cabin right from the factory as part of the G-model line. It comes only in the limited luxury AMG G 63 6×6 model or is produced exclusively for military customers around the world. There is no civilian version available, for love or money.

Above: Above it all: the AMG G 63 6×6 rolls along on six wheels as a luxury off-road supercar; the G 300 CDI DoKa (*below*) from GFG manages with just four.

Anyone who wants a double cabin—also known as the DoKa—with diesel engine will find what they are looking for at G-Class specialist GFG, located in Gotha, Germany. It is built on the G 300 CDI Professional chassis with a wheelbase of 3.40 m and an allowable gross vehicle weight of 4.3 tons. The rear wall divides the driver's cabin from the rest of the vehicle, and the rear part of the long cabin, including the rear doors, is built on separately. At the back, the rear wall of the original short cabin is built on again, to enclose the vehicle. The load area is made of parts for the "open long" military model.

Chassis without cabin (3.40 m)

Primarily intended for military use, the G 270 CDI chassis are supplied mainly to military equipment companies, which use them as a base for making converted vehicles. The Bundeswehr's KSK (Kommando Spezialkräfte) special-forces command units drive special vehicles based on the G 270 CDI chassis. They are driven as fast and heavily armed emergency vehicles in Afghanistan.

Left: Utilized by many of the world's armies: the G chassis with an ambulance superstructure

Right: The double cabin is the rarest G model.

This G was built on a chassis base with a 3.40 m wheels, using a workshop truck body. The vehicle is used as a service vehicle for desert car rallies.

Wheelbase 2.40 m

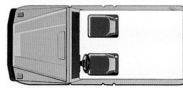

Two seats
open off-road vehicle / panel van

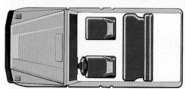

Five seats:
open off-road vehicle / station wagon

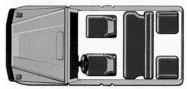

Seven seats: station wagon

Wheelbase 2.85 m

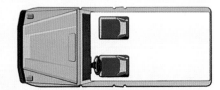

Two seats: panel van

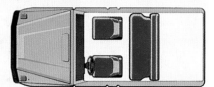

Five seats: station wagon

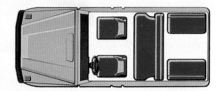

Nine seats: station wagon

This shows just the car seating arrangements that are approved in Germany, but other arrangements were also manufactured.

Chassis with cabin and chassis with cabin 6×6

Different versions of the G 300 CDI 6×6 were produced for the Australian and Swedish armies. The larger vehicle load capacity with low vehicle height was one of the arguments for the 6×6 G. This makes it possible to easily transport the G by air.

Pickup 6×6

The G 63 AMG 6×6 is an additional version of this vehicle body, and at 170 vehicles manufactured, it is not such a rare one. The concept for this vehicle was to design it entirely as a "fun vehicle for cross-country driving"; the load area, which starts too far back, is not intended for transporting seriously heavy loads.

In China blue: Mercedes has put the 300 GD back in the limelight for the fortieth anniversary of the series.

4. The Technology of the G-Class

Above: The inner life of
a classic

Right: The switches for
the locking differentials

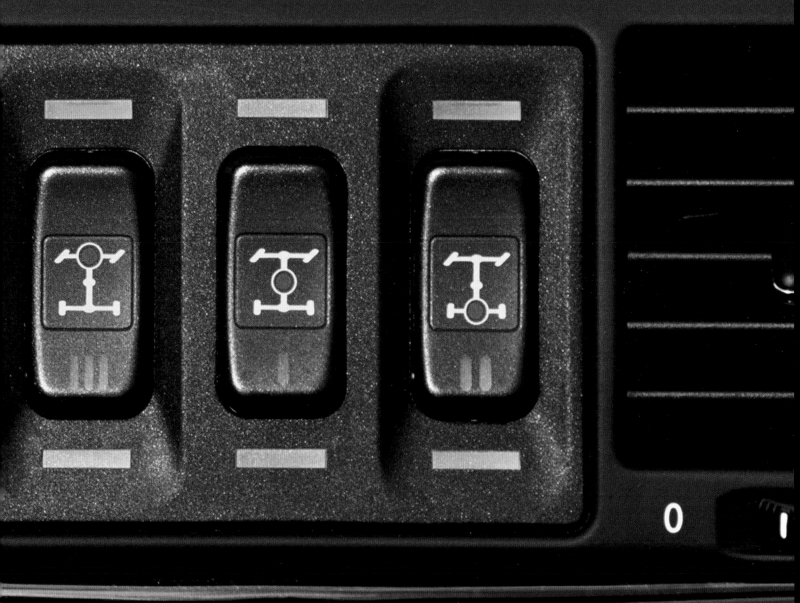

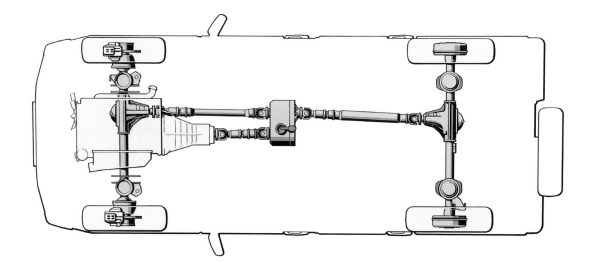

Permanent all-wheel drive has been a feature of the W 463 and W 461 since 2003 (starting with the C 270 CDI).

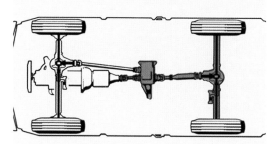
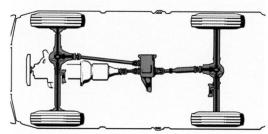

Selectable all-wheel drive on the W 460/461/462

SUV Technology

The data provided in this chapter for the G-Class refer to the standard vehicles; if it refers to technically modified vehicles, the data may differ from this.

All-wheel drive is the most important feature that a vehicle must have to make it capable of driving off-road. It is simply irreplaceable when it comes to driving in deep ground or sand or when it is necessary to tackle a steep incline.

The W 460/461 has selectable (or "on-demand") all-wheel drive with a no-slip differential. The W 463 series, on the other hand, has permanent four-wheel drive with a central differential in the transfer case and associated 100 percent locking. Both transfer cases (460/461 and 463) are fully synchronized so that the gear reduction can be engaged while driving.

Ground clearance is (almost) as important for SUVs as all-wheel drive is. An SUV should have at least 20 cm of ground clearance below the lowest point of the vehicle. Especially if you are driving on rough terrain or through places where there are big stones, a good level of ground clearance is a prerequisite for mastering the route. All the G models have at least 21 cm of air between the lowest point of the vehicle (the axle differential) and the road.

The **angle of slope** is important when you are driving over uneven terrain. Only a large angle of slope (at least 35° in the front and 25° in the back!) will allow you to drive up steep inclines (dunes, rocks, hills, mountains). The G-Class angles of slope are at least 38° in the front and 31° in the rear. These are fantastic values.

The **ramp angle** should also be as large as possible. A large ramp angle (at least 20°) prevents the vehicle from "touching bottom" when you are driving over hills, rocks, or dunes. The Mercedes G ramp angle is a remarkable 27° on the short-wheelbase model and a respectable 23° on the long-wheelbase model.

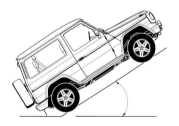

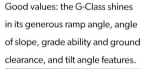

Good values: the G-Class shines in its generous ramp angle, angle of slope, grade ability and ground clearance, and tilt angle features.

Above: Generous ramp angles and axle articulation are important to keep you moving forward when driving off-road.

Right: The gear reduction is engaged by using the second gearshift.

The **axle articulation** is an important factor in an SUV. A wider axle articulation range is essential to compensate for very uneven terrain. In an SUV, this value should be around 20 cm. In the G-Class vehicles, the axle articulation ranges between 25 and 29 cm, depending on the model.

Any SUV that takes itself seriously should also be able to drive through water, so a high fording depth is a prerequisite for driving. Anyone who wants to be able to drive his or her SUV without having to compromise needs a vehicle that can make its way through even longer distances through water of a considerable depth without any fuss. The fording depth specified by

Mercedes is 50 cm; it is also possible to get a vehicle with 70 cm of fording depth without any problem. The G-Class can be driven in water up to 125 cm deep if it has been properly made ready by a qualified mechanic. The necessary equipment is installed right in the factory on specialized military models.

The **off-road gear reduction ratio** is a central feature of any SUV. It makes it possible to considerably increase the starting torque and is therefore absolutely necessary on difficult terrain, but above all when driving with a trailer over easy terrain. The G-Class has an extremely short overall reduction ratio of about 4.1:1.

Having a **ladder frame** is the only way to effectively protect the aggregates on any SUV. The ladder frame furthermore gives the SUV the necessary stability. SUVs must be able to withstand external impacts, such as what happens when they come into contact

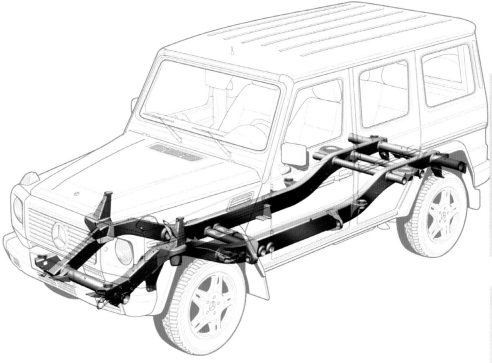

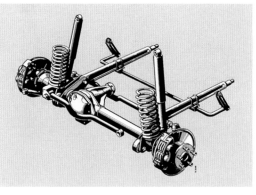

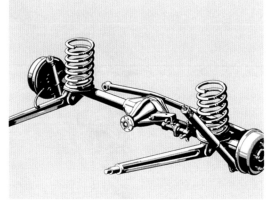

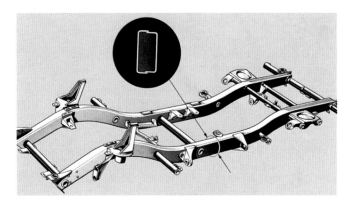

Far right: The rigid axles and coil springs on the W 460/461/462

Left: The solid ladder frame forms the backbone of the G-Class chassis.

with rocks or trees, without needing repairs or even becoming unfit to drive after a collision. Survival in the wilderness is closely associated with having such vehicle capabilities, and any immobilized vehicle (in such places as in a desert, on a steppe, or in a polar region) can lead to critical situations.

The extremely stable ladder frame is constructed of two long, box-shaped, parallel beams that are fastened together by means of several tube-shaped crossbeams. The lengthwise beams themselves are constructed of two U profiles each, one "telescoped" into the other and then welded together. The cross beams are inserted through holes in the lengthwise beams and then welded to them. The chassis is bolted to the frame in eight places.

Coil springs make a generous axle articulation possible and provide for excellent comfort when driving over rough terrain. The G-Class chassis, with its long-stroke, well-damped coil springs, makes it possible to drive at high speeds even over difficult terrain, and ensures that the vehicle holds the road extremely well on level ground. The springs can be adapted to various requirements by using different designs (e.g., hard, soft/long, short) as necessary. Just by using the original springs from the Mercedes range, this car can be modified—to increase the load capacity and to give it a higher or lower suspension setting—for any kind of use. The original springs are designed progressively and will not easily break through. Suspension lifts from the vehicle accessories market are linear and uncomfortable, because they act extremely hard from the first spring deflection millimeter and still "jack it up" because they don't get harder toward the end of the spring travel. They make it possible only to accommodate larger wheels. The driving dynamics suffer from this.

Rigid axles always guarantee the same ground clearance, they are stable throughout and technically uncomplicated, and, above all, they interlock well. The disadvantage is in how much they weigh. The inertia of the unsprung mass hampers fast driving off-road and leads to loss of comfort during normal street driving, in comparison to an independent wheel suspension.

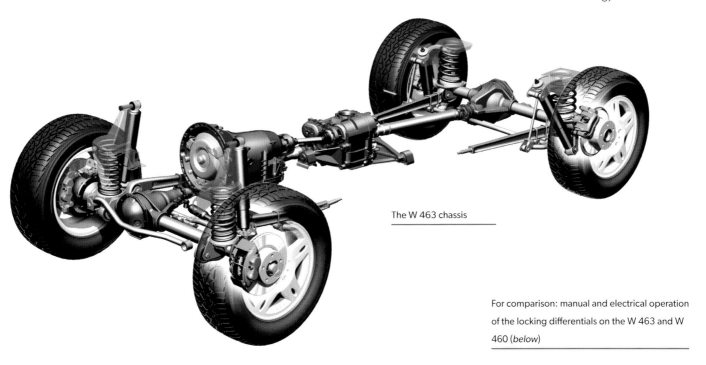

The W 463 chassis

For comparison: manual and electrical operation of the locking differentials on the W 463 and W 460 (*below*)

However, the rigid axles on the G-Class, which are steered by trailing arms, offer a very good comfort level and road-handling quality. Besides, the design is extremely stable.

Locking differentials are indispensable on rugged terrain. Without them, an all-wheel-drive vehicle is usually powered by only two wheels; in this situation, the differentials distribute the power of the engine to the wheels with the least traction. If by chance the two wheels diagonally opposite each other happen to have no traction (they are spinning), normally you cannot move forward. To prevent this effect, many so-called SUVs have differential brakes that slow down the spinning wheel. SUVs that want to be taken seriously, on the other hand, have additional (or alternative) 100 percent locking differentials that can be engaged "on demand." The locking differentials mechanically establish a rigid connection among the wheels. Some SUVs come with a device that makes it possible to lock only the transfer case, and other models come with two locks (one for the transfer case and one for the rear axle). However, on the Mercedes G, three 100 percent locking differentials are standard equipment.

Off-road and on the road, a powerful **engine** is an absolute necessity. Various engine concepts work very well; the most important thing is a high torque, even at low speed. Turbo-diesel and gasoline engines with large engine displacement are ideal. Compared to diesel engines, gasoline engines have more spontaneous pickup; diesel engines, on the other hand, shine in their high torque and lower fuel consumption. It really doesn't matter whether they are diesel or gasoline—V8 engines are synonymous with top performance.

Down-to-earth outfitting: this 300 GD from 1986 has its original crash protection and Recaro seats.

All models in the W 463 series benefit from having appropriate motorization. The new generation of engines is optimally designed for the G-Class's requirements. In the W 460/461 series, the 280 GE and 290 GD Turbo in particular provide convincing evidence of their capabilities with their appealing driving performance off-road and on the normal road.

An **automatic transmission** is superior to a manual transmission in many situations. This is most obvious when climbing a high sand dune, because the automatic transmission shifts down virtually without interrupting the traction at all, making it possible to conquer the obstacle with ease. Starting up on gradients is likewise much easier with this type of transmission than with a manual, and in addition to this are the advantages when driving with a trailer. An automatic transmission is also prone to less wear and tear than a manual, but at the same time it weighs more and is much more expensive to repair.

An automatic transmission has proven its worth in the G-Class. Since the introduction of the 290 GD Turbo, only G models with automatic transmission have been available on the civilian market. A special feature of this type of transmission in the W 460, and an advantage it has over other makes of car, is that a Mercedes G with automatic transmission can also be towed away and tow a trailer without creating any problems. It was generally possible to use vehicles of this series to tow trailers until 1990. The so-called secondary pump, which is driven by the cardan shaft, provides the necessary oil pressure in the transmission to do this. As soon as the vehicle to be towed reaches a speed of 40 km/h, it shifts to speed stage 2 in order to be able to continue driving under its own engine power.

What is the ideal **weight** for SUVs? Basically, a light car is better for driving off-road than a heavy one is. However, if you need this vehicle for rescuing other vehicles or for towing a trailer, an empty weight of about 2,000 kg is a clear advantage. The G-Class, weighing in at 1,740 to 2,500 kg, is clearly one of the heavier SUVs and comes with all the advantages and disadvantages that such a weight entails.

On normal roads, no one wants to be without the advantages of an **antilock braking system** (ABS). On the other hand, ABS is dangerous when driving off-road because it extends braking distances to an extreme extent. On an SUV, therefore, the system should be selectable or "on demand." On the G-Class (W 463), the ABS switches off automatically when the central differential lock is engaged. Older vehicles of the W 463 series have a switch for this function. On the W 461, the ABS is turned off when four-wheel drive is engaged.

Little by little, more and more electronic driving aids are gaining ground, even in the SUV range. An **Electronic Stability Program (ESP)** and the Brake Assist and **Electronic Traction Program (4ETS)** have been features of the G-Class series since 2002. The 4ETS is active up to a speed of 60 km/h. The G copes well with these aids in all everyday situations, but when the road gets really rough, they are deactivated when the central locking differential is engaged. Then the G can give full play to its trump cards, such as the three 100 percent mechanical locking differentials.

The 350 GD Turbo chassis

G-Class Technology in Detail

The **engines** for G-Class vehicles all originated in the Mercedes-Benz passenger car series; at the same time, these engines have been adapted with corresponding modifications to such components as the intake and exhaust manifolds and the adapted oil pans. In addition, the performance of the gasoline engines was reduced in favor of their torque. In particular, drivers of G-Class vehicles that had been manufactured up to 1993—the engine range was changed starting from this time onward—did not always think that their requirements for performance had been met to the extent they desired, and had their vehicles upgraded with V8 engines.

Owners of a G-Wagen of the W 460/461 series with a diesel engine have been making do in a similar way. Those who do not own a 290 GD Turbo diesel and are not very enthusiastic about the performance of their G-Class—which is actually acceptable given the high vehicle weight—have the option of making more power available by installing a turbo-diesel engine.

In the W 463, the least powerful engines (250 GD and 230 GE) were no longer available as early as 1993, and only six- and eight-cylinder engines (apart from the G 270 CDI) were available in the engine range for this model series. The 500 GE V8 special series from 1993 offered the ideal power source for the G-Class. Starting in 1998, a V8 went into series production in the G 500, which was supplemented by the G 400 CDI in 2001.

Manual transmission in the W 460/461: The four-speed transmission in the W 460 comes from the Mercedes Transporter van series. Along with the five-speed transmission on the "Wolf" (the military model), which also comes from the Transporter van series, it is considered very robust. G-Class transmissions always differ from the passenger car and van transmissions because of their special drive flange. The aluminum five-speed transmission for the 280 GE and 300 GD from the W 460 series, made by Getrag, with the long fifth gear (0.87:1), comes from the W 123 car series and is somewhat more responsive.

The five-speed transmission used in the military model has a short first and a direct fifth gear (1:1). When converting this very stable transmission from the Transporter series, the original gearshift gate must be retrofitted. The five-speed transmissions on the 230 GE, 250 GD, and 290 GD are identical to the W 463 transmission.

All W 463 vehicles have a five-speed transmission as standard equipment. This is the transmission series known from the W 460 (230 GE and 250 GD), which

can also be found in the six-cylinder models of the W 124 passenger car series.

Automatic transmission in the W 460/461: The four-speed automatic transmission on the original G model is based on a version from the passenger car series, which in turn was derived from the automatic transmission on the W 123. The first G models with automatic transmissions were delivered starting from 1981.

In the W 463, the four-speed automatic transmission comes from the W 124 passenger car series and has been modified for installation in the G (including the oil pan). The electronically controlled five-speed automatic transmission, which likewise comes from the Mercedes passenger car series, made the G the first SUV outfitted in this way. The fifth-gear ratio is 0.83:1.

With the G 320 CDI, the new **seven-speed automatic transmission** was introduced in the G. From 2007 onward, it was also installed as standard equipment in the G 500 (M 113). Only the G 55 AMG supercharger and the W 461 would continue to be delivered with the five-speed automatic transmission.

The **nine-speed automatic transmission** (NAG3) is installed as standard on all W 463 A vehicles (G 500, G 63 AMG, and G 350d). The new direct control allows faster and smoother gear changes. The transmission is designed for a maximum torque of 1000 N m. The wide gear spread of 9.15 makes it possible to lower the engine speed level.

Despite having two additional gears, the transmission requires the same installation space its

99

Unique in the world: the fully synchronized G-Class three-shaft transfer case. The lockable transfer case (VG 150) from the W 463 is the heart of the G-Wagen's all-wheel-drive technology. Alongside it is the five-speed manual transmission of the 300 GE, the last mechanical manual transmission in the W 463.

predecessor had and, at 95 kg (including oil and converter), is also a kilogram lighter.

Transfer case in the W 460/461: The rigid, fully synchronized two-shaft transfer case of the first G-Class generation has a 1:1 ratio and is linked to the manual or automatic transmission via a short cardan shaft. The all-wheel drive, off-road gear reduction, and all locking differentials can be engaged at any time while driving— this is a unique feature. Drivers of G-Class vehicles don't have to stop or even get out of their car, like drivers of other SUVs do, because the fully synchronized transfer case makes this superfluous. The extremely low-range gear reduction (2.14:1) doubles the starting torque and halves the maximum speed. Furthermore, customers were able to order an optional auxiliary drive connected to the transfer case on the W 460. This allows the G to power various auxiliary units with up to 54 hp!

In the W 463: The fully synchronized three-shaft transfer case has a longitudinal differential between the front and rear axles, which enables speed compensation between the two axles. This makes the power train ABS compatible. The primary advantages here, in addition to tension-free driving in all-wheel drive and off-road gear reduction, are the even traction and less driving noise. The drive power is distributed to both axles in a 50:50 ratio. The normal transfer case has a ratio of 1.05:1, while the version for the turbo-diesel and V8 models has a ratio of 0.87:1. The reduction ratio in off-road gear is an incredibly low 2.16:1; the starting torque doubles when the reduction is engaged and the maximum top speed is halved.

The W 463 A has the transfer case with electronically controlled, multiple-disc clutch from the GLE/GLS and X 350d models, with 40:60 power distribution in road gear and 50:50 between the axles

in gear reduction. Power transmission is done via a multiple-disc chain.

Axles: On the chassis, little has changed since the introduction of the G-Class. Two solid, rigid axles are each guided by two trailing arms and one transverse control arm. The forged trailing arm and transverse control arm are mounted in rubber bushings on the frame and axles. Both axles have coil springs; their impact is limited by hollow rubber springs. The different springs available for the G-Wagen are marked with color codes according to hardness and length. This makes it possible to tune each vehicle individually. A stabilizer is mounted on the front axle. On armored vehicles, an antiroll bar is also fitted to the rear axle. There is a hydraulic steering damper on the front axle, which reduces vibration to the steering. The axle ratios are as follows: the differential locks of the W 460/461 are engaged and disengaged hydraulically with the aid of a shift cylinder, with a shift dog mechanically connecting the two driveshafts of the opposite wheels.

W 460/461

3.95:1	(290 GD Turbo)
4.11:1	(optional equipment)
4.37:1	(optional equipment as well as the 230 GE automatic and 280 GE in F)
4.90:1	(230 GE, 280 GE, 300 GD)
5.33:1	(230 G, 240 GD, 250 GD)
6.17:1	(250 GD, Peugeot P4)

W 463

4.11:1	(G 300 Turbo, 350 GD Turbo, G 400 CDI)
4.36:1	(500 GE, G 500, 300 GE automatic)
4.86:1	(230 GE automatic, 300 GD automatic, 300 GE five-gear, G 320)
5.29:1	(230 GE, 250 GD)

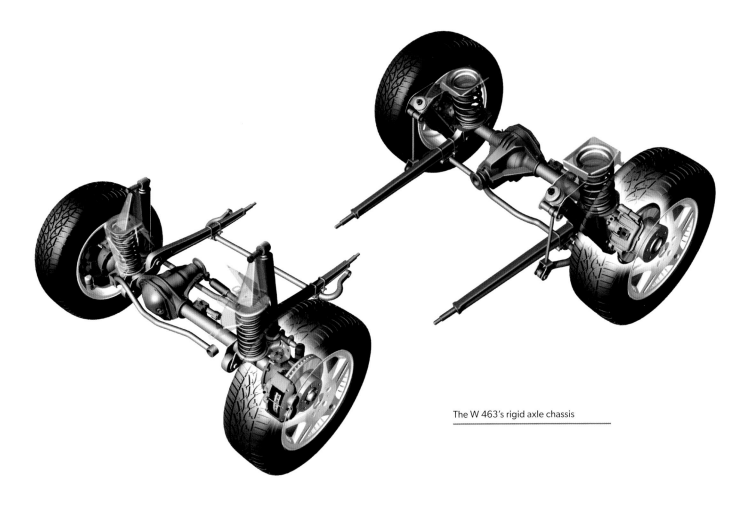

The W 463's rigid axle chassis

W 460/461

3.95:1 (290 GD Turbo)

In the interior, the two levers are pulled upward to do this. On the W 463, the three differential locks function electrohydraulically. They are engaged in the specified sequence (center/rear/front) at the touch of a button on the instrument panel.

Shock absorbers: One twin-tube telescopic shock absorber per wheel provides vibration damping on the G. The original oil-pressure shock absorbers from Fichtel & Sachs have repeatedly proven themselves to be "the measure of all things." The Bilstein gas pressure shock absorbers are stable but a little uncomfortable, especially for off-road use, because it can be very hard to adjust them.

The **brakes** on the W 460/463 feature a load-dependent brake force regulator that distributes two-thirds of the braking force to the front axle and one-third to the rear axle. The rear duo-servo drum brakes are certainly up to date, but those who find them a little too weak can find a remedy: you can retrofit the original rear-axle disc brake from the W 463. The 300 GD and 250 GD models from the W 460 series were equipped with an additional vacuum reservoir. The W 463 series has an additional vacuum reservoir located in the frame, which makes it possible to perform several servo-assisted braking operations, even when the motor is dead. From 1996 onward, all W 463 models were equipped with "Electronic Brake Force Distribution" (EBV).

When the W 463 was presented in 1989, it was the only SUV with ABS, and to this day it is one of the few SUVs that have selectable ABS (on newer G models, it is switched off automatically when the central differential lock is engaged). The most powerful brake system is installed in the G 500 and G 400 CDI; disc brakes all around, internally ventilated at the front.

Various companies offer high-performance brake systems. In addition, many of the sports car brake systems from the Porsche 911 can be installed in the G (same bolt circle). In principle, it is necessary to comply with the TÜV (the German Technischer Überwachungsverein, or Technical Inspection Association) and permit regulations when making such conversions in Germany!

101

This is the way it should be: here this fine black mountain climber shows how axle articulation should work on the G-Class home track on the Schöckl, Graz's local mountain—also known as "the green hell."

A design for the G made available by AMG in 1982. At that time, this model was delivered equipped with 15-inch BBS wheel rims.

G-Class Tires

For the SUV driver, the issue of getting the right tire comes up again and again. Two partial matters have to be taken into account when choosing the right wheel/tire combination. The tire's traction properties—that is, its ability to convert engine power into propulsion by interlocking with the road surface—are of decisive importance. This applies in particular to driving on gravel, on sand, and in slush. Ultimately, the tire diameter also determines the ground clearance and thus the vehicle's off-road mobility. In general, when using rugged off-road tires on the normal road, you should be aware that the rolling noise is significantly louder compared to normal road tires. Many drivers find this really detracts from their driving comfort too much. It also changes the way the tires drive permanently, because the reduced contact area due to the rugged-tread pattern means that the tire can transmit less wheel guidance force, which means that the vehicle response is much less precise.

Besides normal road tires, all major tire manufacturers also include special tires for off-road driving in their product ranges. Decision guides for making the right choice are available from various car accessory companies; these can also explain the potential for conversion if necessary, especially when it comes to using extreme sizes, such as 20 inches and

upward. The ideal tire sizes for off-road driving are 235/85-16 or, because of the greater width, 265/75-16 for the W 463, and 32 × 11.5-15 and 235/85-16 for the W 460. On the W 463, A265/65-18 and 285/60-18 are ideal for off-road driving.

With regard to G-Class rims in particular, it should be noted that it is no longer allowed to fit 15-inch rims on W 463 models dating from 1995 onward, due to the larger brake system. Besides this, the aluminum rims on the W 463 can be driven on the W 460/461 only with wheel spacers, due to a different impression depth (TÜV registration is required).

15 inches

The small 235/70-15 tire size is ideal for vehicles with a long five-speed transmission (such as the Getrag gearbox on the W 460). The 255/75-15 (31 × 10.5 × 15) is the standard tire for 15-inch rims.

A 32 × 11.5 × 15 is the largest tire dimension that can be driven on AMG's 15-inch rims without making any modifications to the vehicle. The rolling circumference corresponds to size 235/85-16. Tires with the designation 33 × 10.5-15 and 33 × 12.5-15 are oversizes that function particularly well on vehicles with short-ratio axles or gearboxes (modifications to the vehicle required).

16 inches

The sizes 205/75-16, 215/85-16, and 225/75-16 are the simplest tires for the G. However, these small tires are always rolling at their performance limit on the road and off-road in extreme situations. Tires of size 235/85-16 are the classic representatives for off-road tires. They are also very widely available in poorer regions.

The 255/85-16, 285/75-16, or 265/75-16 tires have proven to be ideal for the G. Their diameter ensures the vehicle has the appropriate ground clearance for off-road driving, and their width provides optimum grip when the vehicle is running on the road. At the same time, however, it should be noted that you cannot fit these types of tires to a G model without technical modifications, some of which can be extensive. The modifications mainly involve the chassis.

The 235/70-16, 255/70-16, and 265/70-16 sizes work well for road and mixed-use tires on the W 463. The 265/75-16 and 285/75-16 are often fitted with AT and MT (all terrain or mud terrain) profiles.

The 280/85-16 size is available only from Goodyear and Silverstone—both with the same MT profile. These mighty tires are unbeatable in mud, and they dig their way through almost anything, but they also need a lot of space, so the G has to be adapted accordingly. On the road, however, it is impossible to drive on them starting at about 100 km/h! The 37 × 12.5-16 off-road tires work well on portal axles such as the 4×4 Squared when converted to 16 inches.

17 inches

Brabus had very good rims with matching road tires. For drivers of a G 55 AMG supercharger who want to mount traction tires, the usual 16-inch wheels are out of the question because of the size of the brake discs. For such customers, the German companies Extrem Motorsport in Wuppertal and GFG in Gotha are offering a new 17-inch rim in their range, on which the 265/70-17 (32 in.) or 33 × 12.5–17 in. traction tires for track and off-road use can be mounted.

17.5 inches

The chassis with cabin is delivered with 235/75-17.5 tires.

18 inches

The 18-inch size has been the smallest possible rim size available on the new W 463 A and the AMG models since 2005. The 255 and 265/60 are standard road sizes for the G 500 and G 400 CDI. The 285/60-18 has the same rolling circumference as the all-terrain 235/85-16 size.

19 and 20 inches

In 19 inches, the selection of tire sizes is unfortunately very negligible. ORC and Brabus have a few road wheels available in these sizes. The G 55 AMG comes with 19-inch rims as standard equipment starting from the 2010 model year. On the G 63 AMG and G 65 AMG, 20-inch wheels are standard.

21 and 22 inches

Brabus offers rims in these grand "boulevard" sizes. At more than 20 inches, any ability to drive the vehicle for everyday use falls by the wayside. The tires don't have enough sidewall height for the suspension. You can order 21-inch wheels as special accessories for the G 65 and G 63 AMG. Also, 22-inch wheels can be ordered as special accessories for the G 63 AMG (W 463 A).

23 and 24 inches

A range of various 23- and 24-inch sizes are available for the G-Class. The wheel/tire combinations can be obtained from US auto accessories companies, from Kumho Tire Germany, or from AZEV rims. AZEV offers the type R in 10 × 22 inches, which can be produced with a matching bolt circle for the G-Class on request, as well as the US TSW Carlton wheel rim in 9.5 × 23 inches. The US rim from Oasis Type Lundacris is available for the G-Class in 9.5 × 22 and 10 × 24 inches. These wheels cost between 7,000 and 10,000 euros per set with Kumho STX ESCTA tires. The individual TÜV approval needed then adds on 4,000 euros more. Brabus and Mansory offer 23-inch wheels for the W 463 A.

Rims covered with just a thin layer of rubber in 21 and 22 inches

105

The standard rims from Mercedes-Benz (7 × 15 inches)

Left: An 18-inch rim has been an optional feature since 2004.

Right: An 18-inch rim on the G 500, available since 2009

Left: A 19-inch AMG rim, on the G 55 since 2009

Right: The 7.5J × 16-inch five-spoke rim, on the G 320/350 CDI since 2006

From the left: The 5.5J ×
16 inch BBS *Panzerfelge*
("tank rim"), two-piece
since 1980

The 7.5J × 18-inch rim,
on the G 500 since 1999

From the left: The 8J ×
18-inch AMG rim, on the
G 55 2004–2009

From the left: The 8J ×
18-inch AMG rim, on the
G 55 2004–2009

20-inch Brabus rim on
the G V12

8J × 15 or 7J × 15 ZOII
BBS rim, optional
feature on the W 460,
1980–1986

From the left: G 55 with
16-inch "tank rims"
(Canadian army design),
tires 285/75-16 Toyo
Tire Open Country MT

The 17-inch rim from
Extrem or GFG also
provides the G 55 AMG
(large brake) with prop-
er-traction tires.

The 20-inch wheel of the
G 65 AMG offers a more
delicate road design.

Rims

The range of rims available for the G-Wagen is not
particularly lavish but has become much more diverse
in recent years. One special feature is worth mentioning
here: all W 463 models that were delivered without
fender flares have, like the W 460/461, an axle that is
5 cm narrower than other W 463 models. This is why
spacers are required for retrofitting wider rims.

The Mercedes G-Class has the same bolt circle
diameter as the Porsche models 911 and 928, so
the Porsche rims fit all Mercedes G models of the
appropriate inch size. In Germany, of course, this
requires an individual TÜV permit. Brabus, Delta,
CW, AZEV, and ORC also offer various wheel/tire
combinations.

MB/AMG Rims

15″	7J × 15 ET 30 aluminum
	8J × 15 ET 15 AMG aluminum
	7J × 15 ET 63 aluminum
16″	5.5J × 16 ET 63 steel
	5.5J × 16 ET 63 a BBS
	5.5J × 16 ET 38 aluminum
	6J × 16 ET 63 steel
	6J × 16 ET 63 aluminum
	7.5J × 16 ET 63 aluminum
18″	7.5J × 18 ET 63 aluminum
	8.5J × 18 ET 48 AMG aluminum
	9.5J × 18 ET 48 AMG aluminum
19″	9.5J × 19 ET 50 AMC
20″	9.5J × 20 ET 50 AMC
21″	10J × 21 ET 45 AMC
22″	10J × 22 ET 36 AMC

5. Tuning and Sports

Tuning and off-road accessories are also already available for the new W 463 A. GFG has equipped this G 500 for rugged off-road driving.

Right: Both the Mercedes "designo" program and AMG are ready to meet even the most-extraordinary color requests by their customers.

A remarkable cross-breeding from AMG: a W 460 with a W 116 S-Class front. With its 210 hp, the well-tuned 280 GE from AMG was a very potent car.

The 300 hp 280 GE 5.6 from AMG surpassed all other SUVs of its day in terms of performance and driving dynamics.

Factory-Fitted Options for the G-Class

The Mercedes-Benz "designo" program makes it possible to individually tailor a G-Wagen to its owner's requirements. Customers can order special paint and leather colors as well as various applications in fine wood and granite design.

AMG

The success story of this traditional company officially began in 1967, when Hans Werner Aufrecht (A) and Erhard Melcher (M) founded their own company in Großaspach (G), Germany. "Engineering office, design, and testing for the development of racing engines," ran the company description. At that time, the Alte Mühle (old mill) in Burgstall served as the company's headquarters. Customers' growing interest in individualizing the elegant models from Stuttgart and in ever more intensive motor sports activities allowed the company to grow quickly. Today, the high-tech

The G 55 AMG supercharger, with the greatest "passing prestige" on the highway

Individuality à la AMG: "One man, one engine"—each engine is assembled by a mechanic, whose name is immortalized on the unit.

Above: In terms of the technology and designing the interior, as here on the G 55, it is a matter of hand workmanship.

Above: The G 55 AMG supercharger is, according to the BBC, "the coolest car in the world!"

AMG. When the locking differential is engaged in the transfer case, the ESP, ETS, and ABS are automatically deactivated. Only the G-Class driver decides what the car should be doing—something that isn't possible even when driving a Mercedes sports car.

The white paintwork was and remains very popular among many customers from the Middle East and East Asia.

plant in Affalterbach, which has been integrated into the corporate structure of Mercedes-Benz since 1991, is one of the top addresses when it comes to enhancing the performance and refinement of Mercedes vehicles.

At AMG, the company devoted itself to the G model at an early stage, and as early as 1981, shortly after the market launch of the G-Class, the Affalterbach plant had customized conversions for this vehicle type in its range. Hans Werner Aufrecht and his team made numerous pioneering technical achievements reality, such as the installation of Mercedes V8 engines. During the W-460 era (1979–1990), the 280 GE 5.6 from AMG

was the ultimate SUV. The 300 hp V8 engine was able to accelerate the G up to 200 km/h. AMG also offered a mechanical five-speed transmission along with the engine. This monster was available with size 345/60/17 wheels. On request, AMG would also install the entire W 126 S-Class interior, including the seating system, door paneling, and center console, in a G-Wagen.

Later, the vehicle also became available equipped with the 6-liter 331 hp AMG engine. The G 55 and G 55 superchargers laid the foundation for the G model as an everyday super sports car. The next G 63 and G 65 generation continued writing this success story.

Left: Geneva 2017: Brabus shows the spectacular Adventure. A whole range of modifications come from LeTech.

Right: The Brabus G V12

The conversion to the Brabus G V12 was a very complex process, and the result was a very individual vehicle with the prestige of twelve cylinders.

The Brabus G 500

The G 65 AMG, with its majestic 630 PS V12, is the undisputed king of the luxury off-roader sports team. With the G 63 AMG 6×6, Affalterbachers showed that super sports SUVs can sell very well, even if they aren't suitable for everyday driving. The G 63 AMG (W 463 A) is one of the most coveted vehicles in the AMG portfolio, with a delivery time of over one year.

Brabus
The company with the sonorous name has been dealing with tuning Mercedes vehicles since 1977. For the G-Class, Brabus offers a comprehensive package that includes performance, optics, communications engineering, and armoring. Special products that demonstrate the competence of the company from Bottrop include the height-adjustable chassis for the G models and a tuning kit for the G 400 CDI, which will put 310 hp at the driver's disposal after the car has been given this performance "rehabilitation." Thus, Brabus leaves nothing to be desired when it comes to refining G-Class models. The wide range of V12 conversions that Brabus has already made reality, on the basis of the G 500, is almost legendary, initially as the Brabus G V12, then as the Brabus G V12 Turbo, and finally as the G V12 Turbo S, with an incredible 800 hp. On all G V12 models, the transfer case gear reduction is disengaged so that it is not exposed to any risk of "crumbling."

113

A G-Class from ORC with portal axles from Unimog: because it had not been possible to ever resolve some warranty issues, the conversions were bought back.

Most of the G V12s were sold to Russia. In the Brabus catalog, you can find many more or less expensive ways to refine the G even further. In addition to enhancing the performance, we should primarily mention the range of large rims and high-quality ways the interior is outfitted here. But at Brabus, you will seek in vain for any accessories specifically for SUVs.

ORC

This Swabian specialty-tuning company from Holzgerlingen, Germany, offers many interesting modifications for the G model in its product range. By the way, ORC produced the first twelve-cylinder G. All imaginable equipment for motor sports and expeditions is available from ORC. The most interesting ORC conversion was the reequipping of G vehicles with Unimog axles. Because of the portal axles, the "Gmog" has a spectacular ground clearance at its disposal and is equipped with the Unimog's integrated tire-pressure-monitoring system. However, at ORC they also take care of the needs of "normal" G-Wagens: here you can improve them for any particularly rugged driving, such as by installing a double shock absorber suspension, a special brake system, or an antiroll bar for the rear axle. ORC sells mainly accessories specifically for SUVs. In the special ORC Mercedes catalog, you will find everything that an expedition vehicle requires, from a winch to an intake snorkel.

This G 55 AMG with military body was
converted by GFG by installing, among other
things, a 5.5-liter V8 from MKB with 408 hp.

MKB

Anyone who finds that the performance of their
G 55 AMG or G 55 AMG supercharger still isn't
good enough for them can have it improved even
more at MKB in Winnenden. MKB has experience
in tuning up AMG vehicles. Simple options include
changes to the ignition, intake, injection, or exhaust
systems. MKB engines have also proven their worth
in G models used in motor sports driving. The boss
at MKB, Panos Avramidis, learned his craft at AMG;
he will find the right answer for every issue, no
matter how complicated, involving Mercedes engines.
This company will also install manual transmissions
instead of the standard automatic transmission in all
G models.

A W 461 chassis with Unimog axles. This is
likewise a conversion by ORC.

He is back: Arnold
Schwarzenegger
is happy about the
Austrian approach to
electrifying a G vehicle.

With this massive ARB
bumper on the front,
you have no need to fear
any obstacle you might
encounter.

Kleemann

The Danish supercharger specialist Kleemann has also dedicated itself to the G. Using a special supercharger, Kleemann helps a "simple" G 500 (M 113) achieve 460 hp, while the G 55 AMG from Kleemann will move even faster with its 610 hp. Equipped with the Kleemann supercharger, even the G 320 V6 will attain an astonishing 400 hp. Kleemann has already developed supercharger engines for a number of tuning companies and specializes in this type of performance enhancement.

Kreisel

The Austrian electric-vehicle specialist Kreisel has electrified a 2016 G vehicle. A special enthusiast

played a decisive role in the design and development of this type of vehicle: Arnold Schwarzenegger. The G-Wagen, rebuilt during a two-month developmental time span, has a range of 300 km. The liquid-cooled high-performance battery, with a capacity of 80 kilowatt hours (weight: 510 kg), is distributed over several storage tanks under the hood, in the rear in place of the gas tank, and under the entry.

Several electric motors with reduction gears are located directly on the transfer case. The main gearbox has been removed. The drive delivers 490 hp and takes 5.6 seconds to get from 0 to 100 km/h. The vehicle's top speed is 183 km/h. It is possible to charge up this electric car to 80 percent in twenty-five minutes.

A 6×6 in the 1990s cult color of bornite: Schulz converted this G to three axles for a customer in Saudi Arabia even before it became fashionable.

In the 1980s, the tuning virus spread all over the place. Various companies, such as Rainer Buchmann (bb), tried it on the G.

LeTech

Andreas Lennartz has had a very remarkable career in the SUV business. He initially joined ORC as a designer and was responsible there for the most-innovative and most-interesting projects and developments involving the G-Class. These include some motor sports projects such as the Rallye G and M, as well as G models with Unimog axles. After an interlude at the Porsche tuner Gemballa, he founded LeTech in Winnenden, Germany. The

117

The Sbarro Windhawk is based on the Mercedes 280 GE (W 460). The Swiss car designer built twenty vehicles in the first half of the 1980s; one of them as a 6×6 for the Saudi royal family. Most of these cars were delivered with the legendary V8 M 100, with a displacement of 6.9 liters and 286 or even 350 hp (AMG M 100). This makes the Sbarros the kings of engine displacement among the G-Class.

There is LeTech know-how to be found in the G 500 4×4 Squared and the G 63 AMG 6×6. LeTech has developed a powerful tire inflation system for the G 63 AMG 6×6 (*picture at left*).

company developed the portal-axle system for the LAPV 5.4, G 63 AMG 6×6, G 500 4×4 Squared, and G 650 Maybach.

Beyond this, LeTech continued to be involved in rallying, and a G-based rally car came onto the market in the Lennson CC. Four of these vehicles were sold. In 2012, Oliver Koepp and Jörg Sand achieved a tremendous eighth-place finish overall on the 5,000 km long international top-class Silk Way Rally.

The development contracts from Daimler's G Department brought rapid growth to LeTech. In the meantime, LeTech has also been dealing with the restoration of old G models and developing accessories for the new ones.

GFG mbH (Ltd.)

Elaborate bodywork conversions and restorations are the specialty of GFG from Leinatal. The largest "independent" G-Class dealer rebuilds 120 G models each year. Extended pickups and civilianized military G models are just a few of the many modifications done by GFG. It is not without reason that the company name is reminiscent of GFG, which produced the G models in Graz from 1979 to 1981. Managing director Daniel Wiesel is a "Daimler man" through and through. After a year at ORC, he and Jörg Sand founded GFG in Gotha. Today, GFG is the largest dealer for used G-Class vehicles worldwide.

Clockwise, from top left: The GFG 400 CDI comes with long legs and retrofitted Tibus portals and 37-inch wheels. Mansory outfits the G 63 AMG in luxury safari style, and the Opac Contender is also luxurious, with a G 320 to be found in its coupe body.

Mansory

Based on the G 63 AMG, the Mansory "Sahara Edition" has carbon fiber body parts. The vehicle is completely covered in camouflage and has 828 hp, 22-inch aluminum wheels, and a handmade leather interior. The fenders make this G some 40 millimeters (mm) wider. Underride protection is integrated into the redesigned front spoiler. The AMG eight-cylinder biturbo delivers a torque of an electronically limited 1,000 N m.

Opac Contender XG

It was the middle of the 1990s, and nobody had an SUV coupe on their radar (BMW—later hailed as the discoverer of this niche with the X6—still wasn't building an SUV at the time). Really? Nobody at all? The Italian specialist Opac, known above all for convertible tops, was building the Intruder (based on the short G 320) for the French manufacturer Heuliez, which would make a trade fair appearance in 1996. The two-seater had a kind of folding roof like the SLK, which had been introduced at the time. There were also a handful of coupes named the Opac Contender XG from Status & Class in Geneva. The Opac coupe cannot deny its roots: it drives exactly like a G 320, and in fact only the seating position and height are unusual. It is a pure two-seater, and you can actually use the trunk only if you leave your spare tire at home.

119

The OM 603 A is an ideal upgrade for the 250 GD and 290 GD (W 461 and W 463) and the 300 GD (W 463).

The OM 617 A can be readily installed in the 300 GD and 240 GD (W 460).

Do-It-Yourself Tuning

If the engine or transmission on a G model is in need of an overhaul, the idea of installing a more powerful unit will come to mind. Here, however, everyone should be aware that this is a complex operation, requiring not only a lot of special tools but also the necessary expertise and craftsmanship. First of all, because of compatibility, it is advisable to use only parts from the large Mercedes construction kit. Since the current models are well engineered, the following information refers to older G models. For vehicles with a gasoline engine, beyond the most-powerful units of the 280 GE and 300 GE series, it is worthwhile to install a V8 engine. Only the engines of the M 117 series come into question here. The aluminum engines, with 3.8 to 5.6 liters displacement and 204 to 300 hp, are perfect for installation in the W 460/461, using the original installation parts from the 500 GE. To avoid subsequent damage to the oil pan, it is necessary to install either the oil pan from the W 107 (380-560 SL) or the corresponding part from the 500 GE in the V8 engine. In parallel to installing a V8 engine, only a Mercedes automatic transmission can be used for the transmission, due to the high torque. Here the versions from the W 126 (S-Class) are available. The exhaust system can end as a "side pipe" version on both sides, at the height of the B pillar.

For vehicles with diesel engines, it is recommended that they be rebuilt using Mercedes turbo-diesel engines. The choice range includes the 300 TD Turbo (OM 617A, 125 hp) from the W 123, and the 250 TD (122 hp) and the 300 TD (147 hp) from the W 124. None of these engines have ever been installed as standard equipment in a G-Class vehicle. This means that it is necessary to use parts from the passenger car series and from other G models for rebuilding a vehicle. The least complicated option is to install the 290 GD Turbo engine, which was also used in the Mercedes "Sprinter" van and in the E-Class (W 210). Here you can install original parts from the 290 GD Turbo. As is the case for the gasoline models, installing an automatic transmission is also an advantage for the diesel models. Given the high torsional moment of the engines, the manual transmissions prove to be not stable enough. The OM 606 LA is the perfect engine for extreme tuning even on an older G, if you want a diesel. The 3-liter in-line six, with turbo-charging and four-valve technology, comes with electronic injection from the factory but also runs very well with the mechanical pump from the OM 603 LA35. The original pump can also be converted to mechanical if necessary.

In addition, the electronically controlled five-speed automatic can be replaced with manual five- and six-speed transmissions. The OM 606 LA is the last prechambered diesel from Daimler and runs even on bad-quality and impure fuel. It combines the high diesel torque with the joyful revving of a four-valve engine. For "drifting" motor sports, the OM 606 LA can achieve up to 600 hp. Up to 450 hp should be suitable for everyday use. The engine can handle large turbochargers and high boost pressures. You cam upgrade all W-463 diesels built before 2000 with an OM 606 LA with no hesitation. In the W 460/461, the transfer case (VG80) in particular does not tolerate such enormous torque. For such classic cars, more emphasis is now being placed on originality.

If you have decided to convert an engine, it is in any event advisable not to look for a single engine alone, but to buy an entire car as a "parts donor" for the transmission and the many other parts that will have to be installed. If possible, you should of course also take a test drive in the "parts donor"!

Before putting the idea of rebuilding an engine into practice, you should take a look at the axle drive ratio, which must match the engine engineering. Otherwise there is a risk that the powerful engine will be overtaxed; for example, with a 4.9:1 axle ratio. This will then make it unavoidable to get a longer axle drive ratio, which means that the cost of a complete rebuild will amount to more than 20,000 euros, at least half of which is for used parts. No matter how much you might love the idea of such a conversion, it is important not to lose sight of the economic issues, because together with the value of your own G, in case of doubt a used 320 GE or 350 GD Turbo is the less expensive solution.

If the 280 GE engine (M 110) is exchanged for a high-compression M 110 from a passenger car, performance increases from 150 to 170 hp.

Mercedes-Benz offered the Rotzler mounted winch as a optional feature. Several companies offer winches for the G; the most popular are those from the US manufacturer Warn.

On a G 320 (M 104), replacing an engine with one from the AMG C-Class C 36 (W 202) can be done with no problem. This achieves 272 instead of 211 hp through simple engine replacement and adaptation of the engine control unit. In the G 500 (M 113), too, the engine can easily be replaced with the 5.5-liter AMG engine, including adaptation of the engine control unit. This results in about 354 instead of 300 hp; suitable engines can be found in the ML 55 AMG, E 55 AMG, CLK 55 AMG, S 55 AMG, and SL 55 AMG. As for all engine conversions, the G oil pan should also be used here.

G-Class Accessories

Mercedes-Benz offers more accessories for the G-Class than for all the other Mercedes-Benz models, from solid luggage racks, snow chains, and exterior mirrors for recreational vehicles, to impact protection, which is permitted in the EU only on vehicles built before 2008. Exception: the permissible total weight must be at least 3.5 tons.

However, specialist companies have also established themselves in the accessories market, such as Winchindustries in Augsburg, Horn Tools in Austria, or Taubenreuter. An off-road driver will find an excellent selection of high-quality accessories here.

The Taubenreuter company, for example, is the specialist for electric cable winches, which are a particular advantage when driving in difficult forest terrain. This supplier even has a special winch bumper for the G-Wagen in its product range.

The 4×4 Kiefer company in Sasbach has dealt extensively with the G as a touring vehicle and offers a selection of accessories for travel lovers. Hans Kiefer is an enthusiastic G driver himself and is involved in the "community."

121

The three-axle G from the French company De Leotard was brought to the starting line at the Paris-Dakar rally in 1985.

The third axle was powered by rubber belts.

A 290 GD Turbo (FIA T4) service vehicle from ORC for the Paris-Dakar rally

Besides this, US accessory companies and dealers offer interesting G accessories. However, it is always necessary to clarify whether it would be necessary to register these components with the TÜV in Germany.

The G-Class in Motor Sports

The G as a sports vehicle? For many people, the G is more the vehicle for towing their competing horse or their boat to wherever; for others, it is the vehicle to get you out hunting. However, one of the toughest motor sport events of all time had its premiere in the same year the G did. The Paris-Dakar Rally started for the first time on January 1, 1979. By the early 1980s, the Mercedes G-Class had established itself in international motor sports in "the Dakar." Up to today, this event has seen many G models in action.

280 GE Jacky Ickx

Belgian professional racer Jacky Ickx won the fifth running of the legendary Paris-Dakar Rally in 1983 in a Mercedes-Benz 280 GE. In this race, he put his trust in the information from his navigator, the French film star Claude Brasseur. Compared to the vehicles that are entered in the Dakar Rally today, this car was close to being a series-production model.

The six-cylinder engine was tuned to 230 hp at the Mercedes-Benz Untertürkkeim plant.

The enhanced performance was achieved by installing modified camshafts, an intake manifold from the W 126, and an exhaust manifold from the W 116, as well as by higher compression, a fine balancing of the pistons and connecting rods, raising the engine speed limit to 6,750/min., and adding a special exhaust system. In addition to several VDO auxiliary instruments on the dashboard, there was also a switch for adjusting the ignition to adapt to poor fuel quality if necessary. The car had oil cooling for the manual transmission; the original cooler from the automatic model was used for this. Other modifications to make this a motor sports vehicle, such as the hood, doors, and fenders made of lightweight GRP composite, as well as custom-made aluminum components such as the

By 1982, Jacky Ickx and Claude Brasseur had finished fifth overall in a 280 GE in the Dakar (*top*). *At right*, Jacky Ickx driving to victory in 1983.

aerodynamic structures on the front and rear, the engine underride guard, and the tailgate, made this G look like a racing car.

Due to the extreme loads needed for the rally, the vehicle had reinforced (welded from below) axles. Except for the front windshield, all windows were made of extremely light Plexiglas. Inside the car there is a stable roll cage and an additional 200-liter tank. The vehicle has a specially adapted chassis.

As early as 1982, the Ickx/Brasseur team had taken fifth place in a similar vehicle in the Marathon Rally. They would have won but were given a three-hour penalty for bypassing a checkpoint. In 1983, the victory came after an arduous twenty-one days and 14,000 km through desert, steppes, mountains, and jungle. To date, this remains the biggest sporting success of any Mercedes G-Class vehicle. Among the first twenty participants in Dakar at that time were nine other Mercedes G-models! From 1984 to 1986, some daring hobby racers tried to build on this success with highly unusual conversions, from the G-Buggy (KORO) to the G 6×6.

Interview with Jacky Ickx, Professional Race Car Driver

Ickx is a Formula 1 world vice champion, "CanAm" winner, GP winner in Monaco, and many-time Le Mans winner; he won the legendary Paris-Dakar rally in 1983 in a Mercedes-Benz 280 GE.

◼ Mr. Ickx, what do you think of when you look at your 1983 Dakar Mercedes?

I feel that I am twenty-five years younger when I see that car! Before I switched to Porsche, I took part in the Dakar three times, in 1981 in the Citroën CX; that was nothing. Then in 1982 in the Mercedes 280 GE; we would have won back then if we hadn't overlooked a checkpoint. For this we had three hours of punishment and ultimately "only" finished fifth.

◼ That is why it worked then in 1983.

Yes. I and my codriver Claude Brasseur (the French film actor) won. In 1983, we still had to make our way over 14,000 km in twenty-one days (and not like the 9,000 km in fourteen days today). At that time, we slept in our sleeping bags next to the car and ate only out of cans. At the end of the rally, we looked like unshaven, dirty prehistoric men.

◼ How was your vehicle different in 1983 from the one for the previous year?

In 1982 we took a 280 GE and made it as light as possible. The vehicle for 1983 was also optimized at Daimler AG in Stuttgart, for aerodynamics and engine performance. Nevertheless, it was largely a near-series production Mercedes G. We drove with standard chassis with only one shock absorber per wheel, which would be unthinkable today.

◼ Many thanks for the discussion.

Technical Information

Typ: Mercedes-Benz 280 GE Kurz (W 460),
Paris-Dakar, Baujahr 1982

Motor: Engine power: 230 hp at 6,500 rpm, 250
N m at 4,500 rpm
Aerodynamic parts made of aluminum;
hood, doors, and front fenders made of
light GRP

Acceleration: 0–100 km/h: 9 seconds
Braking distance: 100–0 km/h: 40 m
Maximum speed: about 185 km/h
Weight ready-to-drive: 1850 kg
Tires: 235/85 R 16
Price in 1982: about 150,000 DM

The true-to-detail replica of the Jacky Ickx emergency vehicle was built in 2007 according to original plans.

However, they didn't stand a chance against the well-financed factory teams of Porsche, Peugeot, and Mitsubishi. At the same time, the BMW (motorcycle) and Porsche factory teams also trusted the 280 GE as a service vehicle. In 1985, Porsche even transplanted a V8 engine from the 928 S, with 280 hp and 410 N m, into one of their support vehicles (280 GE). This fast service car (190 km/h top speed) drove along with the last surviving Porsche 959 to victory in the 1986 Pharaohs Rally. The V8-G became the second and fastest service car of all time. In 1987, Klaus Seppi, from South Tyrol, finished sixth in the Paris-Dakar in a completely standard Mercedes 280 GE. Seppi then had a 272 hp V8 engine (M 117) with 5.6-liter capacity

Runs well in the sand:

the 280 GE

Above: Alexandra and Daniela Baur in a G-Wagen with portal axles during the "Breslau" rally

Below: Oliver Koepp and Jörg Sand took seventh place in the Baja Germany in 2003 in this G 55.

126

installed at AMG in Affalterbach. In the 560 GE, he took a very good second place in the Pharaohs Rally '87 against the gigantic Peugeot factory team, behind the Finnish professional rally driver Ari Vatanen. Seppi even managed to outdrive Vatanen in two stages. In the 1988 Paris-Dakar, Klaus Seppi was fighting back at the front when an accident knocked him out of the race. In 1989, Seppi started in this event in a lightweight G with AMG 6.0 V8 (330 hp). This car was—just like Clay Regazzoni's sister car—equipped with a carbon fiber Kevlar body and an engine set back by 30 cm. Seppi was able to clinch a stage victory and humiliated the Peugeot factory team with an almost one-hour lead. But there was no overall victory in sight; against the millions spent

by the factory teams, even the fast 560 GE AMG cars of the private teams didn't have a chance. From 1990 onward, the green Mercedes G of the Spanish "Panama Jack" team caused a sensation, first with a 560 GE AMG (W 463) and then with a 500 GE from G-Tech. The green G models were always in the leading field in the Dakar and other Grand Raid rallies.

From 1997 to 2001, the G almost completely disappeared from the scene at any of the RallyRaids. Yet, in popular sports, G models have won almost every trophy since then. The tougher the rally or the trophy, the more likely a G is to be in the lead. For example, Chris Keim (Stuttgart) won the Munich-Carthago amateur rally in 1999 in a 560 GE, and Hans

Christoph Danner from Graz regularly drives a G 55 fast off-road in the Baja Hungary.

127

The G 500, with an
ORC/Schmude GRP
body, is light and fast.

Sometimes with only
minor modifications, G
models have proven to
be very successful dri-
ving in rallies.

This G 30 CDI AMG (W 463) is one of the lightest Mercedes G-based rally cars, thanks to its lightweight construction throughout, using GRP parts, Plexiglas windows, and a much-shorter frame. The vehicle has a 3-liter, five-cylinder AMG diesel engine from the C 30 CDI AMG (C-Class).

Impressions of the Sahara stage during the Munich-Carthago Rally. Something that looks so simple requires a high level of concentration.

E. Baur (ORC Stuttgart) won the fast Berlin-Breslau amateur rally in 2000 in his lightweight 560 GE. ORC has already produced another lightweight G for this customer. A competition version of the 560 GE was also manufactured according to FIA-T3 regulations at MGS in Alpen, Germany, in 2001; this vehicle made its debut driven by Oliver Koepp from Munich in the FIA Dubai Rally 2001. Koepp had a new FIA-T2-G built at ORC in 2002; with its MKB engine, the car won the El Chott Rally in Tunisia right off the bat. In 2003, Oliver Koepp, with the author as codriver, won sixth place in the Baja Germany—and they ended up as the best amateur team. Koepp finished second in the El Chott in 2003. So the G has not reached the end of its motor sports career by a long shot.

G-Class Custom-Made Designs for the Toughest Rally in the World

A special contribution to the subject of aerodynamics: this exotic G-based vehicle was at the start of the 1985 Paris-Dakar.

The 280 GE that Jacky Ickx drove in the Paris-Dakar in 1983, specially prepared by Mercedes G specialist Heinrich Wangler, had an engine tuned to 220 hp and various aerodynamic components made of aluminum, including an air deflector at the rear to prevent turbulence. The white 280 GE short station wagon with Texaco paintwork had no problems during the demanding rally, apart from a defective valve. By the way, Heinrich Wangler has been in charge of the G models of Mercedes-Benz France for the Paris-Dakar Rally for four years.

The special Porsche conversion of the 280 GE for the Paris-Dakar Rally, in blue-and-white Rothmans paintwork, was driven by Porsche engineer Roland Kussmaul. The 280 GE long station wagon got a 5-liter Porsche V8 four-valve engine with 280 hp under its GRP hood starting in mid-1985. The very compact engine comes from the Porsche 928 S4. The Rallye-G had an empty weight of 2,330 kg (3,000 kg when fully loaded) and a top speed of 190 km/h.

Since the bolt circle diameter of the rims of the G-Wagen is identical to that of the Porsche, 16-inch rims from the Swabian sports car manufacturer were also used.

The 280 GE that Klaus Seppi drove in the Paris-Dakar was still almost a standard model in 1986, but by 1987 the gray-and-white "Fercam" Mercedes was fitted with carbon fiber Kevlar parts and a 5.6-liter V8 engine (M117) at AMG. This was followed in 1988 by a V8 unit (6.0-liter capacity, 331 hp), also modified by AMG, and in 1989, the engine-transmission unit was moved 30 cm back to achieve better weight distribution. This G with the "middle engine" was extremely fast and competitive. While the engine came from AMG, further conversion work was performed by a specialist company in Italy.

The first G-Class of the Spanish "Panama Jack" team for the Paris-Dakar adventure in 1989 was an almost-standard 280 GE long station wagon. Another vehicle of the Spanish team was a W 463 long station wagon with a 5.6-liter V8 engine (M 117) built by AMG in 1991. The green G delivered 300 hp, and the doors and hoods were made of GRP. The car weighed 1,900 kg, ready to race.

The spearhead of the team from 1993 onward was a short W 463 with a four-valve V8 engine (M 119),

560 SEC Turbo: A very unusual vehicle was created in France for the 1988 Dakar Rally. Based on a 280 GE long, an off-road-capable S-Class coupe was built. The C-126 body is made of GRP; it has a tailgate and flip front. Under it lurks a 5.6-liter V8 M 117 with two turbochargers and 450 hp. Unfortunately, the vehicle broke down during the rally.

The "Panama Jack" team put their trust in a 280 GE, a 560 GE AMG, and a G 500 G-Tech.

131

The 2002 Tunisia Rally. The tire pressure control system is easy to see.

which had a capacity of 5 liters and came from the Mercedes 500 SL (R 129). In this configuration, the elaborately rebuilt 350 hp vehicle was very competitive.

For the Paris-Dakar models from 1984 to 1987, the French company KORO used a 280 GE with a light GRP buggy body.

During the same period, various G models with three axles were also built in France and ran in the Dakar—but without any notable success.

Oliver Koepp started in a Lennson CC in Baja Germany.

Lennson CC Rally Raid

Four of these rally cars were built between 2008 and 2010, two by LeTech, one by GFG in Gotha, and one by Team Haltos in Mühlhausen. The blue GFG vehicle driven by Ingo Kaldarasch from Schwerin won the GORM—German Off-Road Rally—championships in 2009 and 2010.

In the yellow LeTech vehicle, Munich's Oliver Koepp and Cologne's Jörg Sand took eighth place in the 4,000 km long "Silk Way" Rally 2012 in Russia, with its top international field of competitors. That was the biggest success for the Lennson CC.

Bottom right: The fuel tank in the rear of the T2 G 55 Rallye from ORC

The "Kitcar" was largely based on the current G 500, but the chassis was heavily modified; for example, with a four-link axle connection. The Panhard bars were saved, which was beneficial for the axle articulation. However, the car lost steering precision and required a daring and experienced driver.

132

Other Sports Versions Based on the G-Class

The UAE Desert Challenge 560 GE driven by Oliver Koepp made its debut in Dubai in 2001. This car, in its red-and-blue AEG paintwork, was extremely fast but was still slowed down by its teething problems. Thomas Döhler drove the AEG car in the Baja Italia 2002.

The FIA T2 G 500, vintage 2002, driven by Koepp represents the most extreme interpretation of a Rallye-G model so far. The vehicle has an incredibly easy-to-swallow Fox special suspension, with 2.5-inch shock absorbers that allow 30 cm of spring travel. It also has a GRP body and a 390-liter tank, which is located in the middle of the vehicle.

The Belgian Jacky Loomans converted a G 400 CDI for the Dakar Rally; he contested the rally with the diesel racer in 2002 and 2003. Loomans also relied on Fox suspension technology.

Trial

The longtime chairman of the German Mercedes G Club e.V., Heinrich Wangler, has been driving an open 560 GE (the "knobbly tiger") very successfully since 1983 in the German and European Off-Road Trial Championships (European Champion 1989).

The German company Seitz in Vaihingen/Enz (MAN truck agency) converted some G models to 500 GE and 300 GD Turbo between 1982 and 1987. The company head, Rolf Seitz, was the many-time winner

Frank and Stefan Stensky swirl through the sand during the German Off-Road Masters in the Lennson CC.

The elaborate chassis technology in the T2 G 55 from ORC illustrates the high technical level of the competition vehicles.

The "knobbly tiger"
driven by trial European
champion Heinrich
Wangler

of the German SUV championship in a 500 GE and European champion in 1988.

Heinkel 280 GE

The Paul Heinkel car body construction company in Dettingen made some of the short 280 GE vehicles even shorter during the 1980s (1984 to 1986) (length 3.88 m instead of 4.10 m). Both the frames of the open G and the vehicles' bodies were cut through and made shorter. These vehicles had an advantage in trial competitions because their wheelbase was reduced by some 22 cm (2.18 m). Besides this, the ground clearance was increased to 25 cm and the angle of slope was also improved. The Heinkel G was lighter than a series G (280 GE: 1,770 kg), and it therefore accelerated faster and was more agile (turning circle 9.35 m). Due to the short wheelbase, the Heinkel G also had a tendency to oversteer quickly, which demanded a skilled driver. At least two of the Heinkel G vehicles were later rebuilt with 5-liter V8 engines.

This rally vehicle has a spring travel of 30 cm. Three powerful shock absorbers from FOX Suspension (US), two 2.5-inch main dampers, and a small stop damper for the axle are at work on each wheel. There are also two spiral springs doing their job per wheel. With a combat weight of 2,100 kg, all this effort is necessary to be competitive in off-road rallies. The car has a 5.5-liter AAAG V8 engine (M 113). It performs with 420 hp in the "open" model and 300 hp with the air volume limiter prescribed by the FIA motor sports association.

The T1 G 270 CDI took sixtieth place in the field of 166 cars at the 2005 Dakar Rally.

Oliver Koepp driving in the UAE Desert Challenge in Dubai

Dakar participant: the 300 GE was there at the Dakar Rally in 1992.

6. G-Class Markets and Customers

Almost 2,000 km through the Outback: on the occasion of the introduction of a right-hand model in 2011, the 350 Bluetec took the old Viehtrail Canning Stock Route through Australia.

Versatile: the charging
options on the long sta-
tion wagon model

Here's one standard feature that actually gives
you options. The second-row seats fold forward
in a 60/40 split, so you can accommodate up to
five passengers, or nearly 80 cu ft of cargo, or a
variety of combinations in between.

In its twenty-five years of production time, the
G-Class has sold over 175,000 units to date. The
previous production record was reached in 2002
with 8,700 vehicles. The reason for the later record
was the high level of demand in the North American
market, where the G-Class was introduced only in
November 2001. From the very beginning, military
orders played an important role in G sales, but to
date, far more civilian G models have been sold than
military ones.

The G-Class has one of its most famous customers
in Rome, more precisely in the Vatican city-state.
During his term of office, then Pope John Paul II
was usually driven around in his Mercedes 230 G
"Popemobile." The most specialized feature of the
vehicle is a transparent, bulletproof, open glass cabin.

The Popemobile: from 230 G to G 500

The 230 G went down in history as the "Popemobile."
The car, painted a mother-of-pearl color, accompanied
Pope John Paul II on his travels around the world.
Mercedes-Benz first made this vehicle available to the
pope for his 1980 visit to Germany—initially on loan.
The G-Class was chosen because the pope's car also had
to travel routes that were off the beaten path. The cover
was designed in such a way that it could be removed.
The G-Class built in 1980 was donated to the Vatican in
1982 for the pope's fleet. Besides this, a second, identical
vehicle was made for the pope on the basis of this same
concept. The newer Popemobile, based on a Mercedes-
Benz 230 GE, had the license plate SCV 6.

The first model's twin brother, based on a 230
G, usually carried the license plate SCV 7. The four-

Pope John Paul II had himself driven in a specially made G car.

Right: Pope Benedict XVI was chauffeured in this mother-of-pearl G 500.

cylinder engines with a displacement of 2.3 liters and automatic transmission generated 100 (M 115) or 125 hp (M 102). The 4,392 mm long, 1,950 mm wide, and around 2,800 mm high car was furnished with a particularly comfortable suspension to ensure the pope could ride without vibrations. In 1983 and 1985, respectively, the way the Mercedes-Benz G-Class vehicles were outfitted was adapted to meet the increased security requirements of the Vatican.

During the pope's visit to Austria in 1983, a detail on the exterior of the car was changed: instead of the Mercedes star on the radiator grill, the Puch logo was shining there.

Mercedes-Benz G 500 (SCV 1 Audience Car)

Starting in late 2007, Pope Benedict XVI used an open Mercedes-Benz G 500 long model, so that he could show himself to the faithful during the public Wednesday audiences. The car, likewise painted a mother-of-pearl color, continued the tradition of the Popemobile.

139

The G-Class also works
for fans of ballooning.

Right: In winter road conditions, the all-wheel drive concept proves unbeatable.

The G-Class for Everyday Driving

The G-Class is an ideal family car; the four-door model in particular offers plenty of space for the whole kit and caboodle. In the W 463 long station wagon, you can install three children's car seats in the rear seat (a rarity!). The G's large luggage compartment also offers plenty of space, even when you have already stowed a stroller away.

As already mentioned, the G-Class short model is as long as a VW Golf II, making it just as easy to find a parking space for it in the center of the city. It is also easy to locate your G-Wagen in any very large parking garage, because at almost 2 m high, it clearly towers above the other cars.

Long trips on roads, on highways, and on the slopes are easy to manage in a G-Class. Anyone who gets out of the car after driving 1,000 km doesn't feel totally "knocked out." A G-model with V8 engine, automatic transmission, and cruise control lets you "cruise" very confidently and comfortably on the highway. At the same time, you have to pay attention to the fact that fuel consumption rises extremely quickly starting at a speed of 130 km/h.

As a Leisure-Time Car

The G-Class works really well as a car for horseback riders; with up to 3.5 tons of towing capacity, the Mercedes G can even pull a three-horse trailer. Beyond that, it also offers plenty of space for saddles and other gear. Its modern all-wheel drive can also tow a loaded horse trailer across muddy fields. The short distance between the trailer coupling and the rear axle is ideal for stable driving with a moving load at high speed.

The G-Class is also at home by the water, because its high-level towing capacity, of course, works for towing boat trailers. Pulling heavy boats out of the water, along with their trailers, is one of the easiest jobs

140

for a Mercedes G. Due to its short gear reduction, there is no other car that can take on this job as masterfully as the G-Class. Divers will also appreciate the G's considerable load capacity when they want to transport their heavy equipment.

Hunters have long been regular G-Class customers; they recognize its perfect off-road driving features. In hunting grounds, the G-Class often travels over extreme, rugged routes, which become virtually impassable in damp weather conditions. A Mercedes G will take a hunter practically anywhere. Up to model year 2003, it was possible to order a fold-down ram guard for different kinds of transport jobs from the special-equipment list when buying a new car.

A whole range of options: the G-Class is found at work both in agriculture and forestry as well as at airports.

As a Utility Vehicle

The G shows off its universal capabilities in agriculture. Its loading and towing capacities are decisive purchase criteria for farmers. The W 460 could also be ordered with auxiliary drive. Equipped this way, the G models can take on many types of work that can usually be performed only by tractors.

G-Wagens have also proven their worth on many construction sites over the years, whether as mini excavator tractors, crew transporters, command vehicles, or equipment carriers—the G-Class always offers the right solution.

The G-Class also proves itself in underground mining just as much as in surface mining, regardless of whether it is salt, coal, or another raw material being mined.

The forestry industry also relies on the G-Class, and the more impassable the terrain, the more likely they are to opt for a Mercedes G.

Specialized trades and contractors are another important group of users, because the G-Class is ideal for their line of work. However, quite a few companies shy away from the high purchase prices.

Top left: The G-Class is also used for mining.

Top right: The G Professional as a dumper with a hydraulically moved platform.

Right: The G Professional as a cable-laying vehicle

Below: The G Professional as a tow truck

Bottom right: Well equipped for rugged winter service

Aviation manager Gunther Holtorf retired at age fifty to travel the world in his Mercedes 300 GD (W 460). After traveling 900,000 km and visiting 213 countries, there are no more blank spaces on his map.

As a Touring Vehicle

The more extreme the trip, the more you need the G-Class. Long-wheelbase vehicles drive especially well on expeditions. You can also order the G with all kinds of special equipment for driving in the tropics. The optional equipment from Mercedes-Benz includes an expedition luggage rack, bad-road chassis, tropical roof, impact protection, ram guard, and bushfire protection. The G also offers the best driving comfort compared to other extreme all-terrain vehicles. Since 2009, the G 300 CDI "Professional" has been back in the Mercedes range, a vehicle that is of particular interest to long-distance travelers and utility vehicle drivers. The electronics have been kept to just what is necessary, and the electronic components have been given a waterproof installation in the center console.

The G 500, with the M 113 engine (296–300 hp), has proven itself as an absolutely reliable travel companion. Thanks to the powerful engine, even difficult routes through the dunes can be mastered without a problem, despite the usual extra load for travel. The G 500 has also shown that it can run without such problems as the electronics issues that occasionally occur in modern cars. The G 500 is actually an ideal travel companion, even into remote regions. For the orthodox faction of electronics deniers, there is still the inventory of 350 GD Turbo and 320 GE vehicles. Manual-transmission fans have to look around for 300 GD and 300 GE models.

Anyone who places little value on performance and comfort, on the other hand, would do very well driving the 290 GD Turbo or 290 GD W 461 models on long-distance trips.

Holtorf maintained his 300 GD in the way he would a commercial airliner. All components were replaced or overhauled when the predicted service life was reached. He as good as never had to complain about the vehicle breaking down.

The German Bimobil company specializes in making campers on a four-wheel-drive chassis. In Oberpframmen, Bavaria, they built an alcove structure called the EX 328, using the G 300 CDI as a base. This cleverly and finely equipped camper cost at least 120,000 euros in 2012 and offered a low-temperature package for conditions down to −35° Celsius, two large beds in the alcove, plenty of storage space, a 148-liter-capacity fresh water tank, and a shower, washbasin, and toilet.

A G for long-distance travel with a large "truck-bed camper"; this model limits your off-road mobility due to its high center of gravity but offers the full comfort of a recreational vehicle, or RV.

The Schmude company has created a particularly unobtrusive yet elegant solution to better adapt the vehicle for travel: the lift-up roof, called a Camptop, makes the G only 8 cm higher when the top is lowered for driving and is also slightly lighter than a steel roof.

As a First Responder's Service Vehicle

The versatile range of the G-Class includes its use as a police vehicle. In Europe, Latin America, and Asia, the G is a service vehicle frequently used by law enforcement agencies. The German police force and Bundesgrenzschutz (federal border guard) were the first major buyers of the Mercedes G. As early as 1980, some 400 G models were delivered to police stations.

German specialized manufacturers (including Binz) offer the G-Class for use as an immediate-response (rescue) vehicle (IRV), a command vehicle (CV), and an ambulance (A) for fire department and rescue service operations. The G-Class can furthermore be found as part of the fleet of all the airport fire departments in Germany. The G's limited interior length is the biggest handicap to using these vehicles as ambulances. Here it is necessary to build a special body or install a body extension on the vehicle. Nevertheless, many G models are in use as ambulances, especially by the military, where they place great value on off-road mobility.

From the very beginning, fire departments have been among the most loyal G-Class customers. Here is a G 320 being used as a command vehicle.

149

Right: Binz ambulance with extended vehicle body

Below: The G as a fire department command vehicle

Right: Binz company ambulance with rear extension

The G-300 turbo-diesel emergency ambulance is already a classic among fire and rescue services.

Above: Ziegler company fire engine with tailgate

Left: Binz company ambulance with "slide-in" piggyback unit

The *Bereitschaftspolizei* (riot-control police) had already obtained a larger contingent of 280 GE models in 1979–1980.

A special kind of 500 GE: this special model from AMG has an effective defense system and provides its occupants with an extremely high level of security in the event of any external attacks.

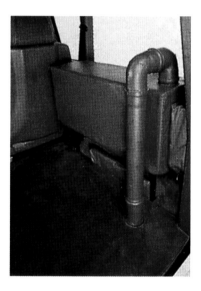

G-Class Armored Vehicles

The German police force utilizes the three-door 280 GE in a special armored model; these vehicles were built during the production years of 1981 to 1983. The "protected special vehicle 3" ("Sonderwagen 3" [SW3]) is a fully armored vehicle (B7) based on a short 280 GE (W 460). The vehicle has air-conditioning and three seats. Special firing vents in the bulletproof glass make it possible to defend the vehicle with submachine guns. SW3s were used by the German police, the Bundesgrenzschutz, and the Bundeswehr. The biggest vulnerability of the SW3 was the engine, which was not powerful enough for the total weight of 3.5 tons. The SW3 was put into service in Germany, Somalia, the Congo, Kosovo, Afghanistan, and Iraq. In 2001, armored G 500s were ordered for use during the EU currency changeover from the national currencies to the euro during the following year—they were used to escort the transport vehicles carrying the valuable cash.

In 1984, AMG made extensive modifications to two G models for the Ritz Hotels in Paris and London. These exclusive vehicles were made longer and given 5.0-liter V8 engines (M 117) and the interior from the Mercedes S-Class. They were then armored and given an active defense system, comprising a shooting slit, four smoke cannons each, a nail gun, and ABC survival kit.

The new armored "Guard" model from Mercedes-Benz is a bit more civilian. The armored G models are some 50,000 euros less expensive to buy than an armored S-Class, thanks to easier options for rebuilding the vehicles. In terms of just the exterior, the "Guard" models do not differ from their nonarmored brothers. The vehicles—the Guard model corresponds to the internationally recognized European protection levels B6 and B7—are usually delivered as G 500 or G 55 models.

In the "Survivor" model, the Austrian company Achleitner is manufacturing an elaborate G-based

The "Guard" G 500 meets the highest safety requirements.

Left: This armored G 500 has bulletproof glass that is 4 cm thick; this meets the standards of protection level B4.

armored vehicle for military use. This universally deployable vehicle features extremely tough armor.

The G 55 AMG XXL: Putin's Special "Spaceship"

The vehicle fleet of Russian president Vladimir Putin includes a whole fleet of Mercedes S and G models. Some G 55 AMGs converted and extended by Binz are used as escort vehicles in the Russian presidential convoy. Their features include sliding doors at the rear. Putin certainly appears to be a Mercedes fan. Daimler AG is also very active in the Russian market, such as with its stake in the truck manufacturer Kamaz. The intention is to manufacture some E, GLC, GLE, and GLS models in Russia.

Thanks to its solid chassis and flat body surfaces, the G is more suitable for armoring than other vehicles.

Civilian Markets

Worldwide, the Mercedes G model (W 463) really has only two serious competitors: the Range Rover and the Toyota (Lexus) Land Cruiser 200. Both of these vehicles play in the same league as the G in terms of price and are designed to be driven both on and off the road. When it comes to luxury SUVs, the 463 and 463 A also compete against the Cadillac Escalade.

The primary competitors of the Mercedes G "Professional" are the Land Rover Defender (production has now been discontinued) and the Toyota Land Cruiser HZJ.

WESTERN EUROPE is already a core market for the G-Class because of Stuttgart's central location. The entire range of G series vehicles is available for sale in European countries, with Germany, Austria, Norway, the Netherlands, and Switzerland being the strongest sales markets. Yet, despite very good sales figures in a any comparison among countries, the G-Class is a car that is seen rather seldomly in Germany, as measured by total car registration figures.

RUSSIA is a primary market for the Mercedes G of the W 463 series. In Moscow, it has become a status symbol among the elite. On the streets of the Russian metropolis, the city where the most G models in the world are driven, the long G 500, G 55, and G 63 AMG models are the most popular.

In **ASIA**, Japan and Singapore are important sales markets for civilian G models. The Japanese order mainly left-hand-drive AMG models.

A relatively large number of G-Wagens are also driven in the Arab states. The Arabs almost exclusively order the top models, the G 55 and G 63 AMG. Even the Saudi Arabian army drives the Mercedes G; they ordered several W 461 (military) V8-powered W 461s from AMG.

The G 55 and G 63 AMG enjoy particular popularity in China, and in 2009 they were the bestselling AMG vehicles in the Middle Kingdom. A

Many of the world's rich and beautiful people enjoy the luxury of the G-Class.

G 55 AMG | SUV

Above and right: The G-Class sells very well in the United States.

new exhaust system has been specially developed for the Chinese market, with the outlets located only on the left side.

In **AUSTRALIA**, as in many countries that drive on the left, the G-Class is rarely to be seen. Anyone who owns one of these rare vehicles cherishes it and takes good care of it. Since the market launch of the G "Professional" as a right-hand-drive vehicle in Australia for the 2011 model year, the G has been seen more frequently there. As a military vehicle, it in any event dominates the street scene "Down Under": the Australian army has obtained more than 2,000 cars.

In **NORTH AMERICA**, incomprehensibly, Mercedes-Benz did not officially offer the G-Class for sale at all until 2001. What sales there were, were made by an independent importer (the Europa company based in Santa Fe, New Mexico), which sold the G-Wagen at astronomical prices. The first 2,600 units of the G (model year 2002) intended for the United States then sold out in a very short time in September 2001. Mercedes increased the number of units, so that it would not annoy its US customers. Today, Mercedes sells more Gs in the United States than it does in Germany.

designo

...awn to the G-Class by its distinctive ...m. But, even among these, there are ...ands a higher degree of singularity. ...xclusive editions distinguished by ... stunning interiors adorned in the ... the most richly detailed wood. The ...d in order to retain its natural grain ... feel. The wood is shaped and ... hand, then matched by the expert ...aftsman. The result is a rare ... of substance, elegance and beauty.

Exclusive
Expressive
Exquisite

SILVER EDITION
Dazzling *designo* Silver paint shimmers under the sun's warm rays. Inside, light radiates from the hand-shaped and hand-polished Natural maple wood, only to be soaked up by supple *designo* Charcoal Nappa leather. A *designo* Silver Edition G-Class is an experience you'll warm to very quickly.

ESPRESSO EDITION
Deep *designo* Mocha Black paint offers a beautiful retreat for admiring eyes to explore. Dive in and bask in the comfort of seats tailored in buttery-soft *designo* Light Brown Nappa leather. The same fine leather even trims the floor mats. Lose yourself in the elegant grain of Natural maple wood polished by caring hands. And as an added tactile reminder of *designo* style, the steering wheel—handcrafted in *designo* wood—puts the fine art of the Espresso Edition in your hands every time you drive.

G500 *designo* editions.

The G-Class is also rare in **LATIN AMERICA**; however, there are some civilian specimens on the road there, especially in Mexico. The G is often to be found in South America as a police vehicle, yet the military model is driven only by the Argentine armed forces.

In **AFRICA**, the G can be found comparatively frequently, but of course not as often as Land Rover or Toyota models. G models are driven by such groups as the German Society for Technical Cooperation (Gesellschaft für technische Zusammenarbeit [GTZ]) or similar German developmental-aid organizations in almost every African country.

There are also enthusiastic G drivers in Australia.

157

7. The "Green Line": The G-Class in Uniform

Leathernecks: the US Marine Corps drives the Mercedes W 461 (290 GD Turbo and G 270 CDI) as an Interim Fast Attack Vehicle (IFAV).

Above: In contrast to the Peugeot P4, the French Panhard G is technically almost identical to the Mercedes G.

Right: The German Bundeswehr Wolf has proven its worth in Somalia, Kosovo, and Afghanistan.

The Bundeswehr "Wolf"

At the end of the 1980s, a major operation to procure vehicles for the German Bundeswehr was pending. Eight car manufacturers, two of them German (Mercedes-Benz, VW), took part in the tender, which ended on March 31, 1987. Mercedes-Benz fielded a 250 GD with shorter axles and a van transmission (with a short first gear) as its candidate.

On the basis of an intensive life-cycle cost analysis, the Bundeswehr decided on the G-Class. The first order (250 GD only) comprised a total of 12,500 vehicles, which were delivered during the period from 1990 to 1998. Every month, 240 cars were produced for the Bundeswehr.

Daimler delivered four different designs of the W 461 series 250 GD "Wolf" vehicles to the Bundeswehr. All models are transportable by air. It is also possible to transport all the models as external loads on a helicopter. The design for the airborne troops (*Luftlandetruppen* [LL]) has two additional lashing eyes on the sides, which allow for quick loading and unloading. The Wolf's onboard power supply voltage is 24 volts, which corresponds to the standard in the German armed forces.

The Wolf differs from the civilian model by such features as its rifle mounts, a lamp for map reading, and a spade mount above the engine, as well as a 24 V socket for jump-starting in the engine compartment. In addition to these features, another essential difference is the very spartan way the vehicle is outfitted. The Wolf was given a very robust construction for its long service life; comfort features were deliberately omitted, something noticeable in the seats and door panels.

The four models of the 250 GD Wolf (open short, open long, long closed panel van, and chassis with "slide-in" piggyback ambulance unit) were outfitted with the standard sets of Bundeswehr equipment to meet the requirements of the respective unit. The various standard sets of equipment are fastened to the vehicle by using lashing rails and can be removed in a short time.

The LAPV 6 (Enok II) is equipped with portals screwed to the G axle.

The German Bundeswehr deploys the LAPV 5 (Enok I).

The open Wolf models, which were fitted with seats in the rear, were almost all retrofitted from 1997 to 2000 with an additional roll bar to protect the passengers.

Some NATO units have been operating G-Wagens (230 G with an X license plate) since the mid-1980s. The Bundeswehr continued to order additional G models in various new designs after 1998.

The Wolves are sold in VEBEG (German government surplus equipment sales) auctions (www.vebeg.de). Some of the vehicles have been cannibalized by the Bundeswehr beforehand, so buying them is not always worth it. The Bundeswehr workshops perform simple maintenance (material maintenance levels 2 and 3 = *Material-Erhaltungs-Stufen* or MES 2 and MES 3) and repairs themselves.

The following models were ordered in the first order:

Open version:
short wheelbase
and short wheelbase, airborne troops version
long wheelbase
and long wheelbase, airborne troops version

Closed version:
long wheelbase
and long wheelbase, airborne troops version

Ambulances:
long wheelbase,
closed van, airborne troops version
chassis (3,120 mm wheelbase) with Zeppelin unit

The recently introduced MES 4 (general overhaul) is performed exclusively by the Mercedes-Benz branches in Hamburg, Leipzig, and Koblenz. In these overhauls, the body is taken off the frame to ensure thorough rust prevention.

The first military order was delivered to the Argentine military. After it became impossible to process a large order from Iran because of the revolution there, the Argentinians got their chance. The vehicles were leased, which led to a crazy anecdote. During the Falklands War, British soldiers captured the Argentine G vehicles, whereupon the South American leasing customer stopped the payments to Mercedes, the reason being that the cars had allegedly been stolen. Subsequently, when the British military wanted to order spare parts for the vehicles from Mercedes in England, Daimler refused to sell them the spare parts, since the cars had indeed been stolen.

When Berlin was still divided, the Allies drove Gs as spy vehicles—the military missions of the British and French secret services drove the long 280 GE model, and the US CIA drove the short 280 GE model. On reconnaissance missions in the former East Germany (the Soviets, for their part, were also on the road in the former West Germany), the cars were equipped with massive ram guards, which made it possible to drive through garden fences and over mailboxes at up to 70 km/h. There were also skylights and curtains behind which the spies could take a nap. For tires, they used size 7.00 R 16 because it was the tire size common in East Germany, to make it possible to replace them quickly if necessary. The members of the military missions at times drove in Wild West style, mostly in the vicinity of military maneuvers, and were quite often involved in accidents.

There was likely an outcry in Daimler's department responsible for compliance with legal trade matters in 2011, after the funeral of North Korean dictator Kim

The Serval is used by the Bundeswehr Command Special Forces (Kommando Spezialkräfte [KSK]), here fully manned with a team (three men).

Below: The Serval, named after an African big cat, has a long range due to its economical CDI engine.

Jong Il. Film footage of the funeral procession showed an entire Mercedes fleet, including a few Gs turned out in military style—despite a strict trade boycott. Apparently, the cars had reached North Korea via a "gray dealer" in Austria and a stopover in China.

Light Infantry Vehicle (LIV)

The Rheinmetall Landsysteme company has developed a "Light Infantry Vehicle" (LIV) and a "Light Infantry Vehicle Special Operations" (LIV SO) based on the Mercedes G.

In the Bundeswehr, these vehicles are called the Wolf "ESK" (the LIV) and the Serval reconnaissance and combat vehicle (*Aufklärungs- und Gefechts-Fahrzeug* [AGF]) (the LIV SO).

The Wolf "ESK"

The Wolf ESK (*Einsatzfahrzeug Spezialisierte Kräfte* = special-forces operational vehicle) is a universally deployable vehicle. A range of modules for transporting passengers and materials or for special transport can be mounted on the rear bed of the vehicle.

The vehicle is armored and can be transported by air. By the way, in a tender by the German armed forces it originally—and probably for reasons of cost

(purchase price)—succumbed to the KMW company's "Mungo" (mongoose), which turned out to be a flop during the mission (Afghanistan).

The Serval "AGF"

The Serval is a light and likewise air-transportable vehicle for special operations. It is also known as the Wolf AGF or LIV (SO). The vehicle is distinguished by its heavy armament and light armor. It is named after the serval, an African big cat.

The superstructure for the Serval comes from the Binz company. The open design allows the crew to dismount quickly and ensures a good all-around view. The Serval can be protected against severe weather with tarpaulins; these are spread over the rollover cage and fastened to the fuselage with a zip fastener. In comparison to the Wolf, the square, removable windshields and the longer body stand out.

For this extremely militarized vehicle, air transportability, a maximum degree of mobility, convincing combat strength, and the fastest possible readiness for action after transport were among the specifications.

The Serval was developed especially for and in cooperation with the German Bundeswehr Kommando Spezialkräfte ("KSK") or Special Forces Command, as

A Serval in sand paintwork at its deployment site in Afghanistan. The vehicle is highly mobile because it can be air-transported in and under a helicopter.

The ESK was designed with ten seats as a personnel carrier, but it succumbed to its competitor, the "Mungo" (mongoose) in the tender.

well as the special-operations units of friendly armies. The French army drives a similar vehicle, a G model under the name of the French Panhard company.

The vehicle is also partially armored to protect the crew from side fire and mines. The Serval has been primarily deployed as part of Operation Enduring Freedom in the mobile ISAF special forces in Afghanistan.

The LAPV Enok

The LAPV Enok (named after a raccoon dog) is a protected military vehicle that belongs to the new LAPV (Light Armored Patrol Vehicle) generation of lightly protected patrol vehicles. It is a special development of the Wolf with special protective equipment (*Sonder-Schutz-Ausstattung*,

or SSA for short). The operational experience of the 250 GD "Wolf" (W 461) was incorporated into the development process. Among other things, this resulted in designing the vehicle with a higher chassis. Because of this, the Enok has better rough-road properties than the armored Wolf (standard set of equipment) and is suitable for use under the toughest conditions.

Compared to the previous Wolf SSA, the Enok is equipped with an armored all-steel passenger cell and offers protection in accordance with the NATO standard level 2. The armor has all-around ballistic protection against armor-piercing assault rifle ammunition up to caliber 7.62 × 39 mm, and Class 2a mine protection (explosion under wheel) against antitank mines with an explosive force of 6 kg.

163

Those who find the Wolf (*front*) with its 84 hp as "not much of a sports car" will have little pleasure with the 70 hp Peugeot P4 (*rear*). Here, both vehicles are on the road in the Kosovo deployment region.

The LAP V 7 is based on a Unimog chassis.

The protection has been tested by the German armed forces and corresponds to the requirements for Class 1 protected command and multipurpose vehicles (*Geschützte Führungs- und Funktionsfahrzeuge*, or GFF for short).

Like the (original) Wolf, the Enok is air transportable by the CH-53G helicopter.

The French Army's Peugeot P4 VLTT (Voiture Légère Tous Terrains)

At the end of the 1970s, the French army was looking for an off-road vehicle.

The contract was won by the Mercedes/Puch G / Peugeot P4 series. The French government's basic requirement was that the contract would be awarded only for a "French vehicle." For the P4 this meant 51 percent Peugeot parts and 49 percent Mercedes and Puch parts. The Peugeot P4 is officially a licensed construction by Daimler-Benz and Peugeot. The engine, transmission, interior, fittings, fabric doors,

top, headlights, and lights all come from Peugeot. The frame, axles, transfer case, and body all come from Daimler and Puch. The first series was given a 2-liter, four-cylinder gasoline engine, and the second series a 2.5-liter, four-cylinder diesel (each with 75 hp).

Due to their low weight (1,895 kg) and the standard locking differential on the rear axle, the vehicles have very high-level off-road mobility. The maximum speed on the road, on the other hand, is quite low at 108 km/h. Delivery of the P4 to the French army began in 1981, and a total of 12,500 vehicles were put into service. The P4 is listed at Mercedes/Puch under the series W 462.

The French army, meanwhile, also has various G 270 CDI vehicles under the flag of Panhard in its fleet.

The LAPV SO KSK

At the 2016 Eurosatory trade fair in Paris, Daimler displayed the Light Armored Patrol Vehicle Special Operations (LAPV SO) in its almost final form. The

Down Under: The order from the Australian armed forces resulted in the 6×6 version of the G-Class; Australia and Sweden operate the G 300 CDI 6×6. The three-axle vehicles combine a large payload with a low overall height and have tire pressure control systems (CTIS).

A camouflaged P4 on maneuvers

Left: The LAPV 6 Special Operations is based on the G 300 CDI.

Right: The interior of the Peugeot P4 can hardly be more spartan.

vehicle was intended to replace the Serval of the Bundeswehr Special Forces Command (KSK). The vehicle, which was developed in cooperation with LeTech, features the 184 hp, 3-liter V6 diesel; dynamic chassis suspension on spring struts, which is based on the "coil-over" principle; and portal axles. Two of them (one as an external load) can be transported by a CH-53 helicopter. The vehicle can carry up to three weapons systems.

Above: The simple 250 GD Wolf with hardtop and radar equipment often runs at the engine's performance limit under a heavy additional load.

Left: Only a few Bundeswehr Wolves came with the wheelbase of the long station wagon.

Below: The 85 hp Wolf as an ambulance with a Zeppelin module calls for a patient driver on the highway.

The G 270 CDI vehicles for the Canadian army have armored rims and large Michelin XCL tires; they have really proven their worth in their deployment in Afghanistan.

The G-Class has stood the test as a military vehicle all over the world. Today it is one of the most sought-after vehicles in the SUV class. In particular, its flexible potential for outfitting, due to the various lengths of its wheelbase, and the armored option are among its advantages. That is why the G is deployed by more than seventy armies. The following countries are among them.

Algeria	G 300 CDI
Argentina	230 G
Austria	300 GD
Australia	G 280 CDI
Canada	G 270 CDI
Cyprus	240 GD, 250 GD, 290 GD
Denmark	250 GD
Germany	250 GD, 290 GD, 290 GD Turbo, G 300 TD, G 270 CDI, G 280 CDI, G 300 CDI
France	Peugeot (P4) with 49% Mercedes parts, G 270 CDI (Panhard)
Greece	240 GD
Indonesia	290 GD
Latvia	G 300 CDI
Netherlands	290 GD, 300 GD
Norway	240 GD, 250 GD, 290 GD
Poland	290 GD Turbo
Saudi Arabia	420 GE AMG
Sweden	G 300 CDI
Switzerland	230 GE (automatic with cat. conv.), G 300 CDI
Singapore	240 GD, 290 GD Turbo
United States	290 GD Turbo, G 270 CDIZypern 240 GD, 250 GD, 290 GD

The Australian army decided on the G 300 CDI 6×6. It can drive 2.2 tons through the most-rugged terrain and fits into the Hercules transport plane.

8. Buying Advice

Even a used G is good for a long-distance trip; here racing driver and Mercedes brand ambassador Ellen Lohr in a G 500 during the 2019 Dakar Rally in Peru.

Form follows function: the timelessly beautiful design of the G continues to delight friends of this model, over and over again.

Like No Other Car

A stable, all-terrain car that can pull trailers weighing 2.8 tons, accelerates from 0 to 100 km/h in less than seven seconds with its powerful V8 engine, and then still can be driven as a convertible. When asked about the existence of such a universally talented car, many car dealers would find it difficult to propose any candidates. Towing vehicle, convertible, sports car, SUV—four cars in one, the G 55 AMG Convertible in any case unites all these seeming opposites. But what else distinguishes the G class from "normal" cars? First of all, of course, the shape, which seems timeless; even among purebred SUVs, such an uncompromising shape has become rare. Its flat windows allow little sunlight to enter the interior, thus contributing to keeping it cool, and they also give vehicle passengers a very good view. The high seating position conveys a sovereign feeling when driving and allows a very good all-around view.

The Mercedes G is one of the last cars that is still largely built by hand. This kind of manufacturing makes it possible to achieve an incomparable level of individualization for each car and ensures its unique quality.

A car that exudes independence and individualism, built for the most-adverse conditions. A car that does not depend on roads or paths, that does not let its occupants down even in the most impossible situations, and that is designed for meeting extreme demands.

Nevertheless, drivers quickly find their way around the G-Class, because everything is just as they are used to finding it in any Mercedes-Benz vehicle.

Which G for What?

W 460 (1979–1991)

Today, the first generation of the G-Class primarily leads an existence as a leisure or purely work vehicle. For everyday traffic, the W 460 is always a compromise today because of its low-performance engines and the all-wheel drive without ABS, which can be engaged only via the transfer case (VG 80). The poor level of comfort also speaks against its use as a first vehicle. In the meantime, many enthusiasts have found themselves taking good care of a W 460 as a classic car. It is always still good for fun and games off-road and a model of reliability. But more-modern G models, meanwhile, offer a better basis for long-distance travel. In addition to low-performance four- and five-cylinder diesel and gasoline engines, there was also the 280 GE. With the 156 hp, six-cylinder M 110, it performs satisfactorily, but with fuel consumption on a par with a 300 hp G 500.

W 461 (1990–2000)

For the W 461, manufactured up to production year 2000, which is largely identical in design to the W 460, the same applies as for the W 460—with the difference that in the end, it had an excellent turbo-diesel engine. The 290 GD Turbo is powered by a 2.9-liter, five-cylinder, direct-injection engine with intercooling. While it has plenty of temperament, the 120 hp G consumes only 10 liters of diesel.

W 461 (2001–2013)

Starting in 2001, the W 461 was initially delivered with the 156 hp, five-cylinder common-rail turbo diesel as the G 270 CDI, and from 2007 onward it was given the 3-liter V6 CDI with 184 hp. Both versions had the most robust five-speed automatic transmission. The second gearshift for the transfer case was also left out of the W 461. Thanks to ABS and the powerful engine, the vehicles work very well for everyday driving. However, the robust exterior conceals the reality that a well-maintained W 463 from before 2000 is certainly the more reliable long-distance travel vehicle. The complex exhaust gas purification system causes failures every now and then (EGR valve), and the delayed response of the engine due to exhaust gas purification is rather a hindrance on difficult terrain. Since the vehicles are relatively rare, they are traded at horrifying prices.

W 463 (1990–2000)

The "golden age" of the G-Class began with the introduction of the W 463. The VG 150 transfer case made it possible to use permanent all-wheel drive and to install ABS (note that until 1992, this was available only as an option). The early W 463s, in combination with the six-cylinder engines, still work very well for everyday driving today. They are also a good choice for long-distance travel. The 300 GE, with a 170 hp, in-line, six-cylinder (M 103) engine, has enough power, and its reliability is simply legendary. The flabby four- and five-cylinder versions were decommissioned by 1992. To do this, the reliable and untemperamental 300 GD with six-cylinder diesel (OM 103 30) is supplemented with the 350 GD Turbo. Its OM 103 A 35 initially caused many problems in terms of cooling, which led to some cylinder head damage. A model update in 1994 fixed the problems. Today, practically all 350 GDs have had the 1994 update.

The successor to the 177 hp G 300 turbo diesel already had an electronic injection pump and transmission control. Despite this, the G 300 turbo diesel works well as a long-distance travel vehicle. The engine is one of the best diesel engines Daimler ever built, has good torque, and is powerful.

Unfortunately, the cost-cutters were already wielding their red pencils on outfitting of the W 463, starting in model year 1991. First of all, Daimler saved on the secondary pump in the automatic transmission. It had been installed on all G-Class automatic transmissions up to that point and made it possible to tow the vehicles if the starter motor failed. Later, the alternator's snorkel fell victim to the red pencil. Starting with the G 320, the alternators have to be thoroughly cleaned after every drive through mud, but even then they just don't

last as long as their predecessors did. With the replacement of the 300 GE, the last W 463 model with manual transmission was gone, to the horror of long-distance travel customers.

Fortunately, corrosion protection got better and better until 2000. However, this changed with the major model update in 2001—with fatal consequences: the model years 2001–2006 are considered extremely susceptible to corrosion. Unfortunately, with the model update, the second gearshift for the transfer case and the storage boxes under the front seats were also omitted. With the CAN bus system, the cars also became technically much more complicated.

W 463 (2001–2012)

The vehicles of the model years 2001 to 2006 are sometimes very susceptible to corrosion and have electronic trouble spots from time to time. The diesel engines can often be aggravating. The G 320 CDI with 224 hp is really reliable. The exhaust gas purification is less complex than the one in the later 211 hp "Bluetec" model. The G 500 with 388 hp is a veritable rocket; it delivers sports car results on the road and offers excellent off-road performance. Both versions of the engine are delivered with the seven-speed automatic transmission. The G 55 AMG supercharger, available starting in 2005, is the "Über-G"—an ultrahard-suspension off-road racing car with a ravishing sound.

W 463 (2012–2018)

With the 2012 model update, the G mutated ultimately into a luxury toy for the rich. The new focus of the demands made on the G-Class can easily be seen by what has happened to the interior. Mercedes makes the greatest compromise on the front bumper. To make space for the numerous radiators for the new turbocharged engines, the sturdy steel bumper had to make way for a GRP part with air intakes. This significantly reduces the vehicles' off-road mobility.

W 463 A (since 2018)

The successor to the W 463 has been consistently developed in the direction of a very roadworthy and foolproof luxury SUV. The W 463 A no longer has very much in common with the original G, but it cleverly conceals this under its confusingly similar shell. The body houses an ultramodern SUV. Even though the hardware provides everything needed for off-road driving, the W 463 A still needs to be retrofitted with various protective parts for really serious driving.

Buying a Previously Owned G Class

The brand loyalty among Mercedes G-Class drivers is remarkable. More than 95 percent of all G-Class drivers would buy such a vehicle again (according to the results of a survey by a German SUV magazine). This level of customer satisfaction speaks in very clear terms.

Anyone who is interested in purchasing a G should be aware, right from the start, that the Mercedes G is an expensive car. This applies mostly to the purchase price and always to the maintenance of this all-arounder. The G is a special, technically complex vehicle and requires precision maintenance. It also consumes a lot of fuel (apart from the 290 GD Turbo and G 270 CDI). Spare parts can often be expensive, and repairs for a G generally cost more than they do for Mercedes passenger cars. Nevertheless, for drivers who drive the G according to its capabilities, it is economical.

There are different ways to buy a used G model. One relatively inexpensive option is to purchase a government vehicle. These are all sold centrally in Germany by VEBEG (the German government's official "recycling" company) in Frankfurt (www.vebeg.de). The company, which was founded in 1951 and has the Federal Ministry of Finance as its sole shareholder, is responsible for the in-trust disposal of all kinds of movable goods. The German Bundeswehr takes vehicles such as the 250 GD (internal designation: "Wolf") W 461 short/open military model, 290 GD chassis with slide-in unit (W 461), as well as the 290 GD Turbo (W 461) and G 300 Turbo (W 463), out of service. Experience has shown that a "Wolf" will cost around 12,000 euros.

The German police force sells 280 GE long (W 460), nine-seaters. It should be noted here that

If well maintained, a used G can become a long-term and faithful companion.

173

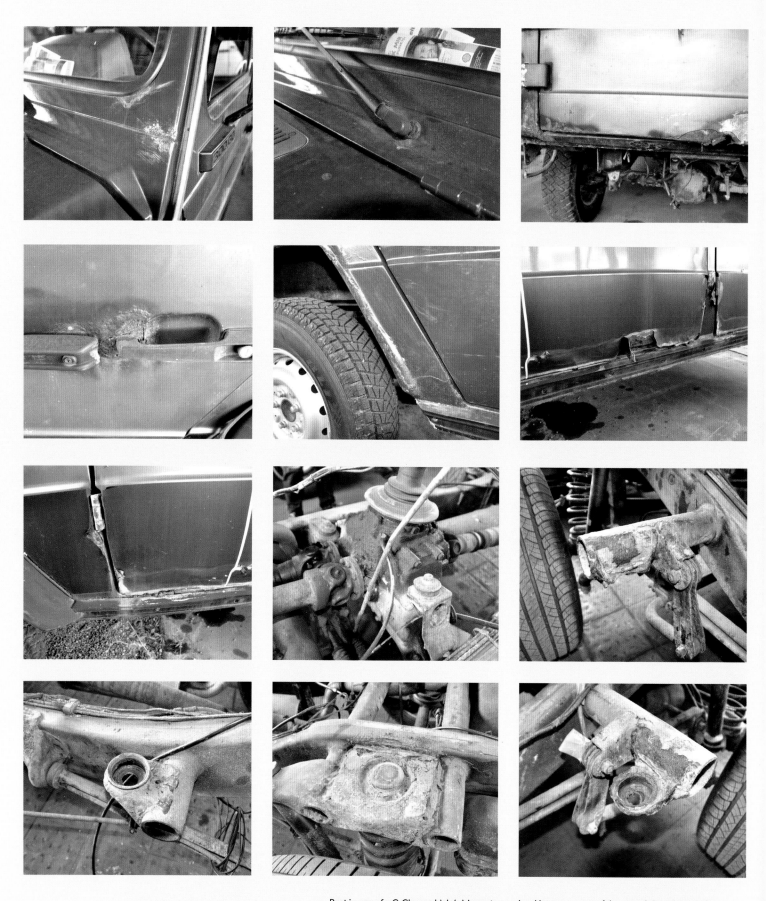

Rust is one of a G-Class vehicle's biggest enemies. Here are some of the neuralgic points on the body of a W 460. The brown pestilence can already impact vehicles starting at four years old. Even the solid ladder frame is not entirely safe from rust at some vulnerable points. It is essential to take a look at spring and damper holders (*lower photos*).

none of the police force G models are equipped with front differential locks. The federal border guard (Bundesgrenzschutz [BGS]) sells 280 GE long models, nine-seaters, and 230 GE short (W 460), seven-seaters. The vehicles are generally in good shape, and all have a hatch in the roof. However, just like the police vehicles, they are almost always out of stock.

The Swiss army occasionally auctions off 230 GE (W 461 military) vehicles—but most of the available vehicles are badly damaged. The G models from the alpine nation are interesting because of their rare axles; all of them are equipped with the long 4.37 axles and have no locks at the front. At the moment, these Swiss vehicles are the least expensive alternative for buying a G.

In France, the French army Peugeot P4s are being scrapped. Since the P4 has the very short 6.17 axles and the Mercedes G transfer case, as well as an identical hood, it would be a good source for spare parts, especially for trial and trophy vehicles.

Mercedes G models are sought after and rare, which is why they are also hard to find as used cars. The most sought-after model is the long station wagon with a diesel engine. The Mercedes-Benz affiliate in Munich

often has a selection of used vehicles in stock. In any case, it is worth taking a look at the advertisements in the Saturday editions of the national newspapers, but of course also at the automotive trade press. On the internet, most G models can be found at www.mobile.de, and there are other portals on the internet that will also be able to give you information. When looking at all the vehicles available in Germany, it is important to note that you will have to invest at least 10,000 euros to purchase a G in reasonable shape. The age doesn't matter here; what matters is the condition of the vehicle.

What should you take a particular look at when dealing with used G models? Proper vehicle maintenance is extremely important for sustaining the value of a G-Wagen. The bodywork on early models, for example, is generally very susceptible to rust in the area of the rear doors and on the sills. The service life of the engines is shorter than that of the same engines in passenger car models. The locking differentials should be checked before buying. To do this, switch on the locks and drive the vehicle slowly in a serpentine pattern. The indicator lights for the locks must now light up. If you can hear cracking noises when driving around tight bends with all-wheel drive engaged on the

A well-maintained G is always worth the money.

175

Iceland—one of the few places in Europe where the G can really live it up. A trip on the volcanic island becomes a driving and nature experience. Caution: a driver should test out unknown waters on foot before driving in.

On this 300 GE, production year 1990, like on many old G-Wagens, the rear door, the rear light holders, the windshield frame, and the sills are rusty.

Engine and transmission parts from Mercedes cars and vans also fit in the G-Class and can be bought inexpensively from used-parts dealers.

W 460/461, this is usually caused by defective drive joints of the front axle shafts.

You will frequently find a leaking crankshaft seal (Borgmann ring) on older models. If this is the case, the loss of oil is usually noticeable because of a corresponding oil stain under the vehicle, at about the middle.

In any case, check the transmission very carefully during a test drive. Is it easy to change all the gears, and do they stay in place when you engage the clutch quickly? Do the gears and transfer case operate smoothly when accelerating and braking abruptly?

The engine should be cold before you start it, and in any case you should drive the engine until it has reached the correct operating temperature, to test the cooling system (radiator, hoses) for leaks. If the windshield wiper shaft wobbles, the wiper bracket is broken. As a result, there is a high risk that water will get in.

Many technical G-Class components can be taken from other Mercedes vehicles for used parts. When rebuilding engines and transmissions from the Mercedes passenger car and van series, it is necessary to keep the G-Class oil pan or make the conversion accordingly.

There aren't many former official vehicles available from army vehicle dealers, such as the 230 G from the federal border guard shown here.

Vehicles on which the hollow spaces have been given additional preventive care, such as this Swiss army G, show hardly a trace of rust even after twenty years.

The Mercedes-Benz Gebrauchtteile Center (GTC; used-parts center) in Neuhausen, near Stuttgart, is a very good supply source for used spare parts. You can find more detailed information on the internet at www. mbgtc.de.

On the German domestic market, people are primarily looking for vehicles with a green environmental sticker or old W 460s that can already be registered as classic cars. All other vehicles are bought mainly from export dealers. The G 400 CDI and G 270 CDI models with retrofitted particulate filter can still get the green environmental sticker, just like all G gasoline engines with a catalytic converter.

Doing extensive restoration work on an old W 460, manufactured between 1979 and 1985, can now be worth its while, since the prices for such old "treasures" are currently rising dramatically.

Restoring an early 300 GE (starting with the 1989 model year) can also make sense: getting 170 hp with a "green" sticker is really something. You cannot get a decent vehicle with a long wheelbase for less than 12,000 euros. Anyone who gets hold of a mechanically well-maintained rusty ruin for 6,000 to 7,000 euros still

has to deal with a budget for bodywork restoration. The companies GFG in Gotha, ORC in Esslingen, LeTech in Waiblingen, and Desert Service in Plauen all perform G restorations.

In the biggest German online car market, there are consistently around 700 to 900 G models available for sale.

The many 250 GD "Wolf" models taken out of service by the German army cannot get an environmental sticker and are often "slaughtered" for spare parts, which brings down the prices for W 460/461 spare parts. However, many "Wolves" will get a second life as classic cars; what you need to do is this: find an old W 460 frame with its registration, as well as an engine/transmission unit that conforms to the production year. When finished, this is a 240 GD, 300 GD (OM 617), 300 GD Turbo (OM 617A), 230 G, or 280 GE model or a 500 GE (M 117) vintage convertible with a performance of 72 to 240 hp. The Magna subsidiary S-Tec near Graz, Austria, supplies spare parts for all Puch Gs. Since they are identical in design to the Mercedes G, this company is able to supply some cheaper spare parts. S-Tec also has its own workshop and always has used Puch Gs available.

179

9. Driving Techniques

The new G-Class W 463 A in the hands of a master: test driver Erwin Wonisch, who unfortunately died in 2018, knew and mastered the vehicles from Graz like no other. The driving tips in this chapter naturally all apply to all G models.

Spectacular drives through water are no problem for a G model—especially when, as here, the experienced test driver Erwin Wonisch is at the wheel.

Whether old or new—every G cuts a fine figure off-road.

Right side: Getting close to nature is part of the off-road driving experience.

182

In a Mercedes G, its owners have acquired the best vehicle imaginable for off-road driving. But even the best chassis is useless if you can't handle it professionally. In the following, we provide useful tips for the proper way to handle G-Class technology. To put the theory into practice, it is necessary to keep practicing. To do this, there are driver-training courses available from Mercedes-Benz and the Mercedes Geländewagenclub e.V. (Off-Road or SUV Vehicle Club), where you can improve your vehicle control under professional supervision.

Off-Road Driving

Before we go into the subject of off-road driving, let's talk briefly about the philosophy of off-road driving. An all-terrain vehicle should be driven not only for the specific purpose of making your way over the terrain, but also for the general pleasure of driving—with the motto "The pathway is the goal." With this special vehicle, the Mercedes G, its owner has acquired a lot of responsibility. Responsibility not only in relation to other drivers on the road, but also with regard to the way he behaves in nature. The SUV driver should feel part of the whole, but there is a difference between experiencing and destroying. SUV drivers must basically be nature lovers, even if this seems to be a contradiction at first, since their vehicles are not necessarily what society today regards as environmentally friendly. As the driver of a Mercedes-Benz G-Class, you should always be considerate of the local environment and everything that lives there—along with all the fun you are having while driving in the great outdoors.

Whoever makes it to the summit can go any-where: All generations of the G-Class have to pass the endurance test on their home mountain, the Schöckl (*left*). The G 500 4×4 Squared is better suited for open terrain. It has grown a bit too wide for the Schöckl.

In a G-Class, you are very well equipped to deal with all conceivable situations that can occur off-road. Nevertheless, you should never drive off-road alone, but preferably always in a group of two vehicles. The weakest component in a G is easily identified—it's the driver. Excuses such as "It wouldn't go any farther because the car broke down" don't count for anything in the great outdoors. Having a well-prepared driver and codriver before entering difficult terrain is highly recommended. Only those who have mastered the technology can operate it properly.

The uncompromising drive concept of the Mercedes, with its three locking differentials, allows the vehicle to keep driving forward even when only one wheel still has any traction.

When and which function of the G has to be switched on or off to keep the vehicle moving depends on the situation. At the same time, there is a special sequence for operating procedures. On the W 463, for example, first engage the gear reduction, then operate the middle lock, then the rear lock, and finally the front lock. On the W 460/461, the locking differential pull knobs are operated first for the rear and then for the front.

The G-Class is often compared to a chamois because of its ability to climb; slowly and surely it scrambles up every height, and its skills are almost legendary. The G-Class can also move quickly cross-country. Here, depending on the ground it traverses, material wear and tear are much greater—and the risk of accidents likewise increases considerably.

Smaller stones and bumps can be managed between the wheels while driving, but this does not apply to bigger obstacles. Anything higher than 21 cm can damage the G from underneath.

185

Caution is advised when driving at an angle on
uneven ground.

This W 460 can manage the route without a problem.

The G 55 AMG, model year 2011, which costs more than 140,000 euros, is an eye-catcher on any street, but it is also impressive off the beaten path: with 507 hp and a brute torque of 700 N m, the SUV, weighing a good 2.5 tons, shows its true qualities on the test track in Schwerin, northern Germany.

187

Steep inclines, both uphill and downhill, must always be driven along the fall line and in low gear to avoid overturning the vehicle. Never turn the car around when driving on a slope! After an unsuccessful attempt to drive somewhere, the safe way to pull back is to drive in reverse gear along the fall line. Any time you are driving either uphill or downhill, do not disengage the clutch; otherwise the car will lose traction. Above all, you should never drive alone in difficult terrain. If in doubt, explore the unknown sections of the route carefully on foot, because you never know what's coming around the next hill!

The G-Class has a tilt angle of 40° (static). It can be safely driven up to 35°, but depending on the load (roof rack) and tires, the car can also tip over sooner. So be careful! If the G starts to tip over, turn into the fall line immediately to avoid a rollover.

For any extreme off-road driving, what is essential above all is to have the vehicle well outfitted and

carefully prepared. Having your car break down can become a serious problem far away from civilization. The tires are the most important thing, because without good off-road tires, even a G is helpless in difficult terrain. The luggage you take along must be kept to a minimum, because every superfluous kilo that has to be dragged over heavy terrain puts unnecessary strain on the car. This applies in particular to loading the roof racks. What you stow on the roof will sometimes raise the center of gravity considerably. In any case, the luggage must be well secured and firmly lashed down.

Before traveling long distances, you should adapt your G to the climatic conditions of your destination (e.g., frost protection, oil viscosity). When traveling in regions you don't know and where the roads are poor, it is a good idea to avoid the risk of driving at night, if possible.

It is much easier to drive in deep sand if you lower the tire pressure. For G drivers who have not

When driving in sand (*far left*) it is important to adjust the tire pressure. A tire pressure control system (*left*) is the best technical solution; this lets you adjust the air pressure from the cockpit (*below*).

retrofitted their vehicle with a tire pressure control system, this means getting out and letting out some air before driving on soft ground. Tire pressure control systems to retrofit a vehicle are available from ORC in Stuttgart and TI Systems in Neuss, at prices starting at 6,000 euros. Integrated systems are significantly more expensive. It is necessary to maintain the tire pressure at a minimum of 0.8 bar to keep the vehicle driving safely. You should never let the vehicle come to a standstill in deep sand, or an elaborate salvage operation will be necessary.

If this has happened anyway and your G is stuck fast, first you have to dig it out, at least until both axles are free. After you have dug it out, if there is no other vehicle nearby to tow it, drive the car very carefully a very short distance back and forth and "rock" it free. Caution with manual-transmission vehicles: such maneuvers put the clutch at extreme risk, so never let the clutch slip, because otherwise the vehicle will quickly become immobilized. The general rule is that you should operate the clutch only for shifting gears.

The rocking technique can also help to free a vehicle stuck in deep snow. When driving downhill in the snow, the differential locks must be disengaged, since the ABS (on the W 463) is activated only when this is done. When driving downhill around tight curves, the all-wheel drive should be switched off on a W 460 or 461. This is because, unlike on the W 463, there is no speed compensation between front and rear axles when the all-wheel drive is engaged. With this no-slip differential, the G thrusts forward via the front wheels, and this considerably enlarges the turning

When driving in snow, the electronic driving aids in the current W 463 are a great help.

The G-Wagen masters inclines of up to 100 percent (45°), and, on surfaces where it can get traction, even up to 110 percent (50°).

circle. Snow chains should be fitted to the rear axle of the W 460 or 461 and to the front axle of the W 463. However, it is best to drive a G with four snow chains. When it gets really cold, make sure to refuel diesel vehicles with winter diesel. In a pinch, you can add up to 25 percent regular gasoline when you fill the tank, to keep the diesel fuel viscous. In such a situation, fill the tank with the gasoline first to ensure better mixing.

For CDI engines, take note that only petroleum is suitable for diluting diesel fuel; otherwise, lubrication of the diesel injection pump will be impaired, and this will cause a lot of subsequent damage.

When driving through water, always engage the gear reduction and drive slowly, because generating a high bow wave will only pose an unnecessary risk. The doors of the G are watertight, but when preparing for

a drive through water that approaches or even exceeds the maximum 50 or 60 cm fording depth specified by Mercedes-Benz, it is advisable to fasten something over the ventilation openings on the lower door rebate to prevent water from getting into the interior. If you come to a passage through water that you do not know, or if you cannot see the bottom, you should explore it on foot beforehand. The same applies when driving through water, as is so often necessary when driving over terrain: do not stop and do not disengage the clutch! Under no circumstances should you drive so deep into the water that the high-level ventilation openings or the intake opening for the air filter become submerged. If the vehicle gets stuck in water that is too deep, do not open the door, but get out through the side window. In the worst-case scenario, if the engine has sucked in water (water hammer), first salvage the vehicle. Then unscrew the spark plugs (the glow plugs in case of a diesel) and turn the engine with the starter until no more water splashes out of the plug openings. After inserting the plugs, start the engine and—if it is still running—get the G-Wagen to the repair shop on the fastest route possible!

If you have misjudged the terrain situation and the G has tipped over, the vehicle must be put back upright as quickly as possible. To do this, attach the recovery cable from the towing vehicle to the

The extremely low-range gear reduction also helps when driving through water.

Fording a river in
Australia

Even a G has its limits;
driving off-road requires
practice.

upper chassis member of the overturned G. Then the vehicle should be towed, slowly and without jerking it, perpendicular to the lengthwise axle of the horizontal G car. When the car is back on its wheels, it is advisable as a precaution to unscrew the glow plugs or spark plugs and let the engine run with the starter motor. This will force out any oil that may have gotten into the combustion chambers. Then check the air filter for any oil that may have leaked in, check the car for leakage, and fill up any leaked fluids if necessary. After you have screwed in the plugs, the G should then run again. In a vehicle with a turbo-diesel engine, the charge air hoses must be removed, because otherwise, if any oil that has gotten into them, it can also get into the combustion chamber and damage the connection rods or pistons.

Fuel consumption when driving off-road is much higher than in normal traffic. Basically, you should count on using double the amount of fuel that you use in normal driving. Since every liter of fuel that you have to carry along also means additional weight, vehicles with economical (turbo) diesel engines have an advantage here compared to gasoline engines.

The locks cause high tire wear on dry roads, and it is better not to engage them if the vehicle is fully loaded, to prevent damage to the axles. The locks should be disengaged when they are no longer needed to move the car forward. Never engage the locking differentials when driving on solid ground (unless for a functional test).

To ensure that the locks are working properly, they should be functionally tested regularly (an interval of about eight weeks is sufficient).

After driving off-road, it goes without saying that you will clean any dirt off your vehicle and check the

underbody for damage. After driving through water and mud, it is important to apply the brakes briefly to dry the brake pads. If you seriously want to drive a W 463 A for a long time in difficult terrain, you won't be able to avoid making a few modifications. These include a stable steel front bumper and a fixed underride guard for the radiator and oil pan. Some cables or lines will also need to be protected. Due to the 18-inch limit, traction tires should be 286/60 R18 format. Think of getting a full-size spare tire! It may be worth it to add an upper ram guard, because the front is considerably weaker than on the previous models.

The G's chassis reveals its strengths when driving fast over open terrain.

193

Although it certainly is ever more geared toward luxury and road comfort, it can still deliver an outstanding performance off-road: the W 463 A.

The long station wagon model not only gives a convincing performance on the test track but can also easily drive off-road despite its size.

Driving on the Road

In regular traffic, the G-Class is outstanding—in the truest sense of the word—because its height lets the driver sit enthroned above the other drivers on the road. After they get into a G-Class, its occupants are in a different world. Eye level in the G is at 1.80 m, and from above there is a perfect view of the G and everything around it.

The passive safety of the G-Class is at an unusually high level. The extremely stable construction of the entire vehicle can be seen from the fact that the doors close like those on a safe.

The G-Class is a special vehicle for driving on difficult terrain; in view of this, it offers excellent comfort and good road-handling features. Due to its design, its center of gravity is naturally higher than that in conventional passenger cars. Anyone who drives the G appropriately will never encounter problems in everyday life. Starting with the 2002 model year, all G-Wagens are equipped with the ESP driving-stability system, which averts dangerous driving situations even when if they are driven incorrectly. The new W 463 A, on the other hand, is 100 percent uncompromising on the road.

When entering underground garages, make sure that the garage height is at least 2 m. The vehicle height varies considerably, depending on the tires on the car.

Driving while Towing a Trailer

The G-Class is ideal for towing heavy trailers, and 95 percent of all vehicles come equipped with a trailer coupling. Accordingly, all models have enormous tractive performance. The permissible towing capacity ranges from 2,810 to 3,500 kg and goes up to 4,000 kg for trailers with air brakes. The older G models with a lower towing capacity can tow more if the appropriate trailer couplings are used. The G (W 463) can be driven in reduced gear ratio without a rigid coupling, which makes it much easier to maneuver a trailer. The G-Class gear reduction has the lowest ratio of all SUV series worldwide; it gives G-Wagens their enormous starting torque, allowing them to tow even the heaviest trailer out of the water or mud or across fields.

Combined with an automatic transmission, this further reinforces the advantage of a high starting torque. The short rear overhang on the G-Class gives the trailer's leverage only a short lever arm for applying force up to the rear axle. The unrivaled short span (the coupling point is only 85 cm from the rear axle) generates excellent driving stability.

This means that even trailers that wantonly start swaying back and forth will have little impact on the Mercedes G's driving stability, and they can quickly be brought back under control again. The not-insignificant weight of G-Class vehicles is additional assurance that your towing team will operate very smoothly. Vehicles with a long wheelbase offer more directional stability and are also approved for towing bigger loads than short models are, although they are

The G-Class makes an
ideal towing machine.

Horseback riders and
boat skippers especially
value its capabilities.

more difficult to maneuver, especially when driving in a towing "team."

In addition to the ball-head coupling familiar from the passenger car sector, a truck drawbar coupling is also available for the G-Class.

When towing, the G fuel consumption is very moderate, and it will consume only a slightly larger amount of fuel.

This is due in part to the fact that its already moderate aerodynamic values will not deteriorate any more when driving with a trailer.

199

Appendixes

An off-roader's dream: the trim and compact G can sometimes function better on the extremely rustic trails on the Baja California Peninsula in Mexico than the gigantic American off-road vehicles do.

G-Class Model Overview

Motor Serie	Cylinders	Hp	AMG/MKB	Hp	Brabus	Hp
200 GE W 463/460	R4	118			200 GE 2.6	160
230 G W 460	R4	90/102				
230 GE W 460/461/463	R4	122/125/126			230 GE 2.6	160
240 GD W 460	R4	72				
250 GD W 460/463	R5	84	ST Turbo	118	ST Turbo	118
G 270 CDI W 463/Worker	R5	156			G 270 CDI	194
G 280/300 CDI	V6	184	MKB	238		
G 320/350 CDI	V6	224	MKB	265	V6 CDI	265
G 350 CDI Bluetec	V6	210	MKB	265	V6 CDI	265
280 GE W 460	R6	156/150	280 GE	220		
290 GD W 461	R5	95	ST Turbo	120	ST Turbo	120
290 GD Turbo W 461	R5	120			290 GDT	150
300 GE W 463	R6	170	300 GE 3.2	232	300 GE 3.6	238
300 GD W 460	R5	88	ST Turbo	120	ST Turbo	120
300 GD W 463	R6	113				
G 300 Turbodiesel W 463	R6	177			G 300 Turbo	204
G 320 W 463	R6	210	G 36	272	G 320 3.6	275
G 320 W 463	V6	215			G 320 3.8	275
350 GD Turbo W 463	R6	136			350 GD Turbo	177
G 400 CDI W 463	V8	250			G 400 CDI	310
500 GE W 463	V8	240	500 GE 6,0	331	500 GE 5.6	280/300
G 500 W 463	V8	296	G 55 AMG	354	G 500 6.1	400
G 55 AMG Kompressor	V8	476-507	G 55 MKB	600	G V12	710
G 500 (550)	V8	388	MKB	422		
G 500 (M178)	V8T	422			V8T	500
G 63	V8T	571	MKB	680	V8T	800
G 65	V12T	630	MKB	721	V12T	900

Car Bodies W 460/461

			Wheelbases in cm
Short station wagon	Open		240
Short station wagon	Closed		240
Short station wagon	Convertible		240
Short panel van			240
Short station wagon	Open, military model		240
Long station wagon	Closed		285
Long station wagon	Open, military model		285
Long panel van			285
Pickup truck	Long		285
Passengers	Long	Cabin	312
Passengers	Extra long	Cabin	340
Passengers	Extra long	Double cabin	340
Passengers	6x6	Cabin	
Passengers	6x6	Double cabin	

Car Bodies W 463

		Wheelbases in cm
Short station wagon	Geschlossen	240
Short station wagon	Cabrio	240
Short station wagon	Cabrio (elek.)	240
Long station wagon		285
Extralong station wagon	(nur AMG)	329
Landaulet extralong station wagon Maybach convertible	Cabrio Maybach	329
Super long station wagon (Wolf factory full-size pickup only)	400 cm	400
AMG Pickup 6x6	Doppelkabine	340
GFG pickup	Doppelkabine	340
LeTech station wagon	6x6	340

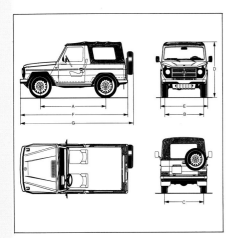

A. Wheelbase	2,400 mm
B. Wheel track front	1,425 mm
C. Wheel track rear	1,425 mm
D. Greatest height (unloaded, including cover)	1,945 mm
E. Greatest width (without side-view mirrors)	1,700 mm
F. Greatest length (spare tire inside, series)	3,955 mm
G Greatest length (spare tire outside**)	4,155 mm
Ground clearance (under the axle) front	211 mm
Turning circle	about 11.4 m
Cargo space (back seat** upright)	765 dm³
Cargo space (back seat** folded down)	1,740 dm³

* when loaded ** available on request

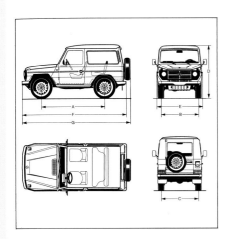

A. Wheelbase	2,400 mm
B. Wheel track front	1,425 mm
C. Wheel track rear	1,425 mm
D. Greatest height (unloaded, without roof luggage rack)	1,925 mm
E. Greatest width (without side-view mirrors)	1,700 mm
F. Greatest length	3,955 mm
G. Greatest length (spare tire outside**)	4,110 mm
Ground clearance (under the axle) front	211 mm
Ground clearance (under the axle) rear	210 mm
Front overhang angle*	36°
Departure angle (without clutch)*	31°
Ramp angle*	25°
Turning circle	about 11.4 m
Cargo space (back seat** upright)	743 dm³
Cargo space (back seat** folded down)	1,730 dm³

* when loaded

These three body designs were the most frequently ordered features for the W 460: the two-door convertible, the closed three-door (short station wagon), and the five-door long model (long station wagon).

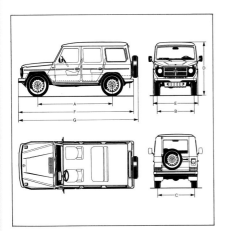

A. Wheelbase	2,850mm
B. Wheel track front	1,425 mm
C. Wheel track rear	1,425 mm
D. Greatest height (unloaded, without roof luggage rack)	1,920 mm
E. Greatest width (without side-view mirrors)	1,700 mm
F. Greatest length	4,405 mm
G. Greatest length (spare tire outside**)	4,560 mm
Ground clearance (under the axle) front	211 mm
Ground clearance (under the axle) rear	210 mm
Front overhang angle*	36°
Departure angle (without clutch)*	31°
Ramp angle*	21°
Turning circle	about 13 m
Cargo space (back seat** upright)	1,340 dm³
Cargo space (back seat** folded down)	2,590 dm³

* when loaded

A heavily loaded 350 GD Turbo has to be rescued in rugged terrain. Its OM 603 A is the last diesel engine with a purely mechanical injection pump. Thus, this car is completely free of electronics.

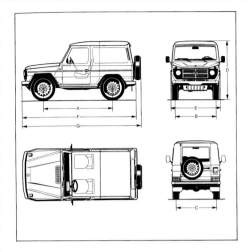

A. Wheelbase	2,400 mm
B. Wheel track front	1,425 mm
C. Wheel track rear	1,425 mm
D. Greatest height (unloaded, without roof luggage rack)	1,925 mm
E. Greatest width (without side-view mirrors)	1,700 mm
F. Greatest length	3,955 mm
G. Greatest length (spare tire outside**)	4,410 mm
Ground clearance (under the axle) front	211 mm
Ground clearance (under the axle) rear	210 mm
Front overhang angle*	36°
Departure angle (without clutch)*	31°
Ramp angle*	25°
Turning circle	about 11.40 m
Cargo space (back seat** upright)	1,870 dm3
Cargo space (back seat** folded down)	2,590 dm3

* when loaded

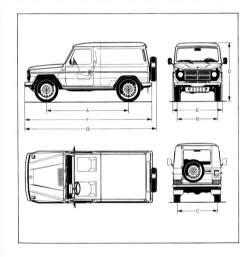

A. Wheelbase	2,850 mm
B. Wheel track front	1,425 mm
C. Wheel track rear	1,425 mm
D. Greatest height (unloaded, without roof luggage rack)	1,920 mm
E. Greatest width (without side-view mirrors)	1,700 mm
F. Greatest length	4,405 mm
G. Greatest length (spare tire outside**)	4,560 mm
Ground clearance (under the axle) front	211 mm
Ground clearance (under the axle) rear	210 mm
Front overhang angle*	36°
Departure angle (without clutch)*	31°
Ramp angle*	25°
Turning circle	about 13 m
Cargo space (back seat** upright)	2,650 dm³

* when loaded

Technical data for the panel van models (short and long) and the ambulance design (*right*) from the W 460/W 461 series

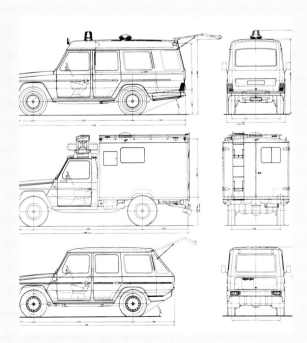

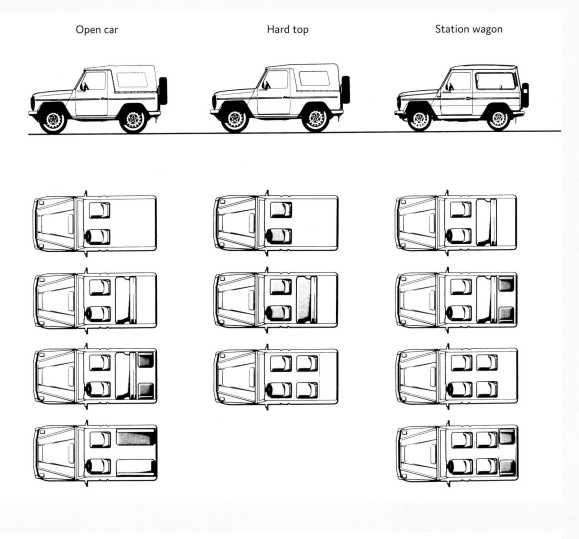

Open car   Hard top   Station wagon

The range of vehicle
bodies for the W 460/
W 461

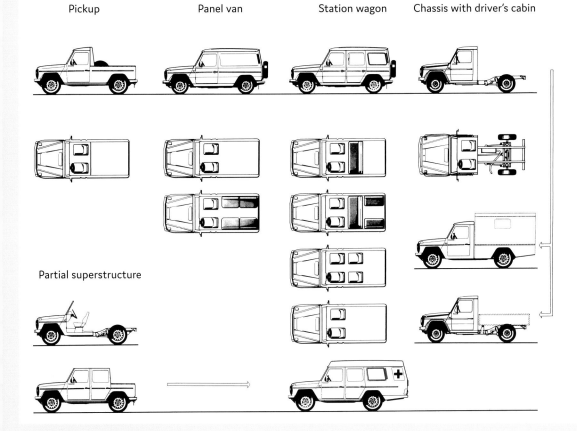

Pickup   Panel van   Station wagon   Chassis with driver's cabin

Partial superstructure

Dimensions of pickup
models (W 461)

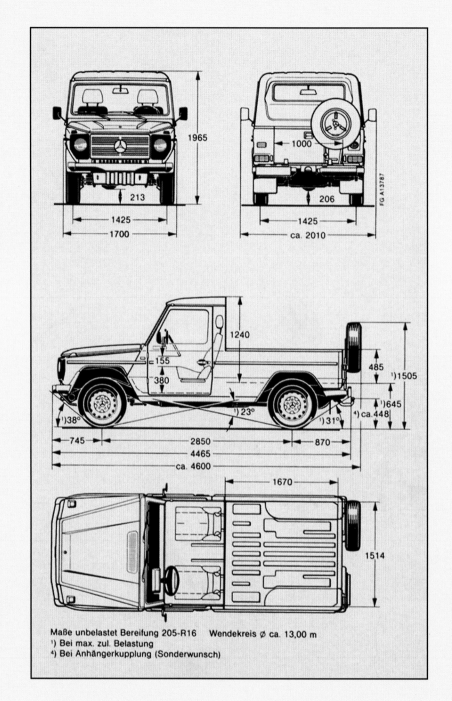

Maße unbelastet Bereifung 205-R16   Wendekreis Ø ca. 13,00 m
¹) Bei max. zul. Belastung
⁴) Bei Anhängerkupplung (Sonderwunsch)

Dimensions of unloaded tires 205-R16   Turning circle about 13.00 m
(1) At maximum allowed load
(4) With trailer coupling (special option)

Different bodies available
for the W 463: the five-
door long version (long
station wagon), the closed
three-door (short station
wagon), and the two-door
convertible

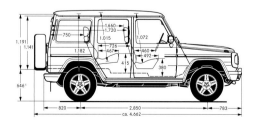

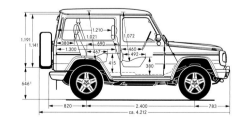

208

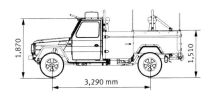

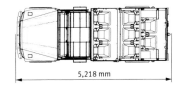

Dimensions of the
W-461 LIV (Light Infantry
Vehicle) model

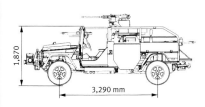
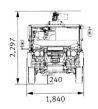
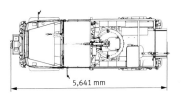

Dimensions of the
Serval (W 461)

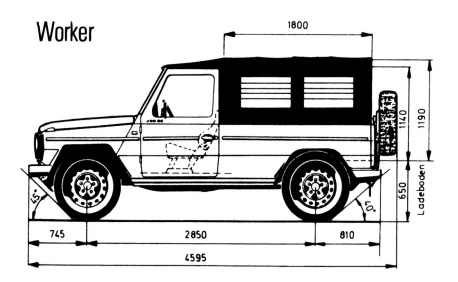

Dimensions of the
Worker (W 461) military
model

Ladeboden = load floor

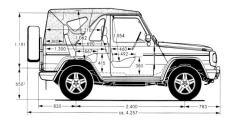

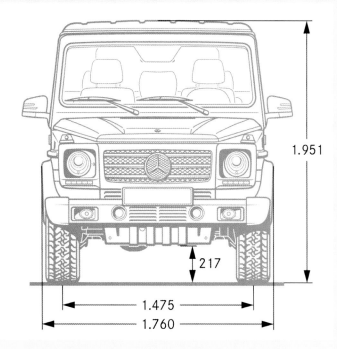

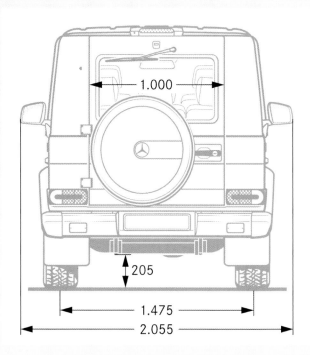

◢ Offroad data Mercedes-Benz G-Class

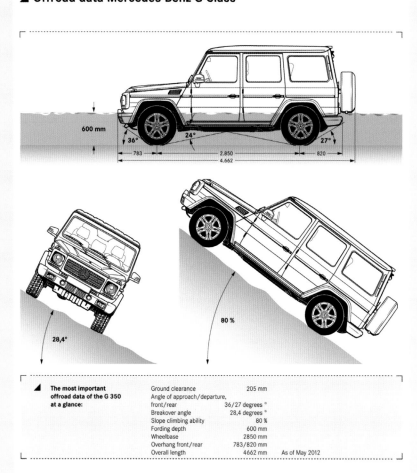

The W 463 as a non-AMG model manufactured from 2012 to 2015 was the last W 463 with a steel front bumper. In the EU, it was no longer allowed to install a ram guard starting with this generation of vehicles (2008 onward). The new rearview mirrors, daytime running lights, and openings in the bumper for the Distronic-Plus sensors compose its distinguishing features. With the G 500 (M 173), the last G engine without a turbocharger was pensioned off, except for 2015.

◢ The most important offroad data of the G 350 at a glance:		
Ground clearance	205 mm	
Angle of approach/departure, front/rear	36/27 degrees °	
Breakover angle	28,4 degrees °	
Slope climbing ability	80 %	
Fording depth	600 mm	
Wheelbase	2850 mm	
Overhang front/rear	783/820 mm	
Overall length	4662 mm	As of May 2012

Mercedes-Benz

Well positioned: this information sheet shows the dimensions and terrain values for the non-AMG models of 2012 to 2015, still with a "good" front angle of slope.

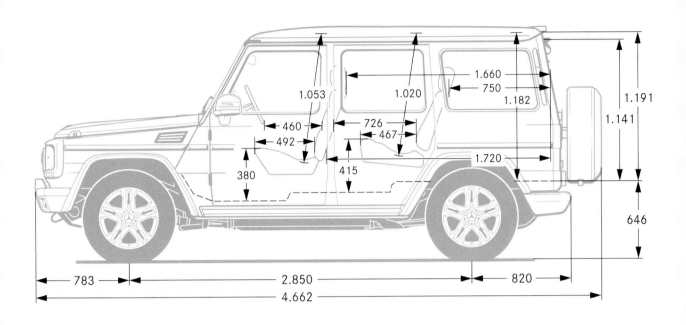

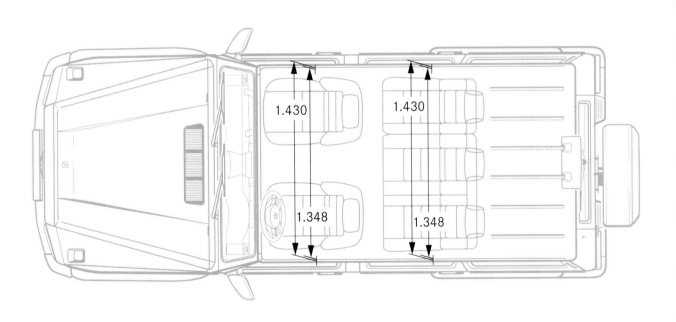

W 460/461

Type	200 GE	230 G	230 GE	240 GD	250 GD	280 GE	290 GD	290 GD Turbo	300 GD
Engine displacement in cm3	1,997	2,307	2,299	2,399	2,497	2,746	2,874	2,874	2,998
Cylinders	R4	R4	R4	R4	R5	R6	R5	R5	R5
Performance in hp	118	90/102	125/122	72	84	156/150	95	120	88
Torque in N m	185	167	192	137	154	226	192	280	172
Fuel system pump	Bosch inject.	Stromb. car-beur.	Bosch K(E) jet.	Bosch diesel pump	Bosch diesel pump	Bosch K(E)-Jet.	Bosch diesel pump	Bosch diesel pump	Bosch diesel pump
Transmission	4 g	4 g	4 g / 5 g / 4 g auto.	4 g	5 g	4 g / 5 g / 4 g auto.	5 g	4 g auto.	4 g / 5 g / 4 g auto.
Axle drive ratio	4.9:1	5.33:1	4.9:1	5.33:1	5.33 / 6.17:1	4.9:1 / 4.37:1	4.9:1	3.95:1	4.9:1
Acceleration 0–100 km/h in s		26	17	32	27	14	26.5	19	27
Braking distance at 100 km/h in m	42	42	42	42	42	42	42	40	42
Top speed in km/h	140	137	150	120	128	160	137	140	130
Curb weight in kg	1830-2000	1740-1950	1830-2000	1850-2020	2000-2200	1900-2050	2000-2080	2010-2200	1885-2080
Allowed total weight in kg	2500-3000	2500-3000	2500-3000	2500-3000	2500-3000	2500-3000	2500-3000	2500-3000	2500-3000
Load capacity in kg	600-900	810-970	600-900	620-900	690-900	610-920	820-910	810-900	620-970
Tow capacity short stat. wg. in tons	2.8	2.81	2.81	2.81	2.81	2.81	2.81	2.81	2.81
Tow capacity long stat. wg. in tons	3.5	3.5	3.5	3.5	3.5	3.5	3.5	3.5	3.5
Fuel consump. liters / 100 km	16	17	16	12	12	19	12	11	13
Tires	205 R 16	205 R 16	205 R 16	205 R 16	205 R 16	205 R 16	205 R 16	205 R 16	205 R 16
Length in cm	411-458	411-458	411-458	411-458	411-458	411-458	411-458	411-458	411-458
Width in cm	170	170	170	170	170	170	170	170	170
Height in cm	195	195	195	195	195	195	195	195	195
Production year	1982-1990	1979-1982	1982-1995	1979-1987	1987-1992	1980-1990	1992-1995	1995-2001	1979-1990

W 463 Gasoline Engine

Typ	200 GE	230 GE	300 GE	320 GE	G 320	500 GE	G 500	G 500/550	G 55 AMG	G 55 AMG Supercharger
Engine displacement in cm3	1.999	2.299	2.960	3.199	3.199	4.973	4.966	5.461	5.439	5.439
Cylinders	R4	R4	R6	R6	V6	V8	V8	V8	V8	V8
Perform. in hp	118	126	170	210	215	240	297	388	354	476/500/507
Torque in N m	185	192	235	300	315	375	456	530	525	700
Fuel system	Bosch inject.	Bosch inject.	Bosch inject.	Bosch inject.	Bosch inject.	Bosch inject.	Bosch inject.	Bosch inject.	Bosch inject.	Bosch inject.
Transmiss.	5 g	5 g auto.	5 g / 4 g auto..	4 g auto.	5 g auto.	4 g auto	5 g auto.	7 g auto.	5 g auto.	5 g auto.
Type Supercharger	1.05:1	1.05:1	1.05:1	0.83:1	0.83:1	0.83:1	0.83:1	0.83:1	0.83:1	0.83:1
Axle drive ratio	4.9:1	4.9:1	4.9:1 / 4.37:1	4.37:1	4.37:1	4.37:1	4.37:1	4.37:1	4.37:1	4.11:1
Acceleration 0–100 km/h in s	18	17	13.5	12	12	11	9.2	5.1	6.8	5.6/5.4/5.1
Braking distance at 100 km/h in m	40.5	40.5	40.5	39.5	39	39.5	39	38.5	39	39
Top speed in km/h	140	145-150	170-175	182	183	185	199	210	215	210 (limit.)
Curb weight in kg	2005-2195	2005-2195	2100-2260	2100-2260	2100-2270	2350	2210-2410	2230-2380	2210-2460	2460
Allowed total weight in kg	2620-3050	2620-3050	2810-3050	2810-3200	2810-3200	2810-3050	2810-3200	2850-3200	2810-3200	3200
Load capacity in kg	615-855	615-855	710-790	710-790	710-780	700	600-690	605-820	590-690	740
Tow capacity short stat. wg. in tons	2.8	2.8	2.8	2.8	2.8		2.8	2.8	2.8	
Tow capacity long stat. wg. in tons	3.5	3.5	3.5	3.5	3.5	3.5	3.5	3.5	3.5	3.5
Fuel consump. liter / 100 km	16	16	19	19	18.5	21	19.5	19	21	24
Tires	255/75 R 15	255/75 R 15	255/75 R 15	265/70 R 16	265/70 R 16	265/70 R 16	265/60 R 18	265/60 R 18	265/60 R 18	285/55 R 18
Length in cm	423-470	423-470	423-470	423-470	423-470	470	423-470	423-470	423-470	470
Width in cm	170	170	170	176	176	176	176	176	176	187
Height in cm	195	195	195	195	195	195	195	195	195	193
Production year	1990-1993	1990-1993	1990-1994	1994-1998	1998-2001	1993	1998-2009	2009-2015	1999-2004	2004-2012

W 463 Gasoline Turbo

Type	G 500 (T)	G 63 AMG	G 65 AMG
Engine displacement in cm3	3982	5461	5980
Cylinders	V8 Turbo	V8 Turbo	V12 Turbo
Performance in hp	422	544 / 571	612 / 630
Torque in N m	610	800	1.000
Fuel system	Bosch Einspr.		
Transmission	7-G-Auto		
Transfer case	0.83:1		
Axle drive ratio	4.37	4.11	4.11
Acceleration 0–100 km/h in s		5.4	5.3
Braking distance at 100 km/h in m	38.5	38	38
Top speed in km/h	210	210 / 230*	230
Curb weight in kg	2,495	2,555	2,585
Allowed total weight in kg	3,200	3,200	3,200
Payload in kg	705	645	615
Towing capacity long stat. wg. in tons	3.5	3.5	3.5
Fuel consump. liter / 100 km	14.5	17.2	22.7
Tires	265/60 R 18	275/50 R 20	295/40 R 21
Length in cm	470	470	470
Width in cm	187	187	187
Height in cm	195	195	195
Production year	2015-2018	2012-2018	2012-2018

*with AMG Driver´s Package

W 463 Diesel

Type	250 GD	G 270 CDI	300 GD	G 300 Turbo	G 320/350 CDI/ Bluetec	350 GD Turbo	G 400 CDI
Engine displacement in cm3	2497	2688	2996	2998	2987	3449	3997
Cylinders	R5	R5	R6	R6	V6	R6	V8
Performance in hp	90	156	113	177	224/210/245	136	250
Torque in N m	154	400	191	330	540/550	305	560
Fuel system	Bosch diesel pump	Bosch diesel pump	Bosch diesel pump	Bosch diesel pump	Bosch inject.	Bosch diesel pump	Bosch diesel pump
Transmission	5 g	5 g auto.	5 g / 4 g auto.	5 g auto.	7 g auto.	4 g auto.	5 g auto.
Transfer case	1.05:1	0.83:1	1.05:1	0.83:1	0.83:1	0.83:1	0.83:1
Axle drive ratio	5.33:1	4.38:1	4.9:1	4.37:1	4.37:1	4.37:1	4.11:1
Acceleration 0–100 km/h in s	27	14.1	23.5	14.5	9.5	17	9.9
Braking distance at 100 km/h in m	40.5	39.5	40.5	39.5	38.5	40.5	39.0
Top speed in km/h	128	162	140	165	177/180	152	187
Curb weight	2,015-2,05	2,275-2,400	2,035-2,225	2,115-2,240	2,260-2,445	2,220-2,350	2,370-2,520
Allowed total weight in kg	2,620-3,050	2,810-3,200	2,620-3,050	2,810-3,050	2,850-3,200	2,810-3,050	2,810-3,200
Payload in kg	605-845	575-790	585-825	595-810	575-755	530-700	465-680
Towing capacity short stat. wg. in tons	2.81	2.81	2.81	2.81	2.8	2.81	2.81
Towing capacity long st. wg. in tons	3.5	3.5	3.5	3.5	3.5	3.5	3.5
Fuel consump. liter / 100 km	12	11	13	15	13	16	16
Tires	205 R 16	265/70 R 16	205 R 16	265/70 R 16	265/70/16	255/75 R 15	265/60 R 18
Length in cm	423-458	423-458	423-458	423-458	423-470	423-458	423-458
Width in cm	170	176	170	176	176	176	176
Height in cm	195	195	195	195	195	195	195
Production year	1990-1992	2002-2006	1990-1993	1996-2001	2007-2018	1993-1996	2001-2006

W 463 A

Type	G 500 (T)	G 63 AMG	G 350 d	G 400 d
Engine displacement in cm3	3,982	3,982	2,925	2,925
Cylinders	V8 Turbo	V8 Turbo	R 6 Turbo	R 6 Turbo
Performance in hp	422	585	286	340
Torque in N m	610	850	600	700
Fuel system	Bosch dir. inject..	Bosch dir. inject.	Common rail	Common rail
Transmission	9 g auto.	9 g auto.	9 g auto.	9 g auto.
Transfer case	1:1	1:1	1:1	1:1
Axle drive ratio	3.45	3.45	3.45	3.45
Acceleration 0–100 km/h in s	5.9	4.5	7.4	6.9
Braking distance at 100 km/h in m	38	37	38	38
Top speed in km/h	210	220/240*	200	210
Curb weight in kg	2,429	2,460	2,485	2,485
Allowed total weight in kg	3,150	3,150	3,150	3,150
Payload in kg	721	690	665	685
Towing capacity in tons	3.5	3.5	3.5	3.5
Fuel consump. liter / 100 km	13.8	16.5	11.7	11.9
Tires	265/60 R18	275/50 R20	265/60 R18	265/60 R18
Length in cm	482	486	482	482
Width in cm	193	193	193	193
Height in cm	197	196	197	197
Production year	since 2018	since 2018	since 2019	from 2020

*with AMG Driver´s package

W 461 Professional

Type	G 270 CDI	G 280/300 CDI
Engine displacement in cm3	2,688	2,987
Cylinders	R5	V6
Performance in hp	156	184
Torque in N m	400	400
Fuel system	Bosch inject.	5 g auto.
Transmission	5 g auto.	5-G-Auto.
Transfer case	0.83:1	0.83:1
Axle drive ratio	4.37:1	4.37:1
Acceleration 0–100 km/h in s	14.5	12.5
Braking distance at 100 km/h in m	39.5	39.5
Top speed in km/h	160	160
Curb weight in kg	2,410-2,540	2,410-2,540
Allowed total weight in kg	3,500-4,300	3,500-4,300
Payload in kg	1,020-1,890	1,020-1,890
Towing capacity long st. wg. in tons	3.2	3.2
Fuel consump. liter / 100 km	10	12
Tires	225/75/16	225/75/16
Length in cm	464	464
Width in cm	176	176
Height in cm	206	206
Production year	2003-2007	ab 2007

You can get to the most extraordinary places in a G-Wagen, such as here in Baja California, Mexico.

Clubs

■ The Mercedes G-Club e.V. (reg. assn.)

Der deutsche Mercedes-Benz G-Club e.V. wurde 1987 von The German Mercedes-Benz G-Club e.V. was founded in 1987 by sixty G-Class drivers in Stuttgart and today has about 1,000 members. Their annual meeting, held in Germany, is a major event for this association of interested people. The club also organizes long-distance trips in their SUVs and driving seminars. The long-distance trips have already taken G-Club members to remote dream destinations as far away as Mexico, Australia, and Mongolia. Trips to North Africa are an integral part of the annual event program.

By the way, Heinrich Wangler was chairman of the Mercedes-Benz G-Club until 2017. He worked at Mercedes-Benz from 1977 until his retirement in 2007. When he joined the company, he was part of the technical staff entrusted with developing and testing the G-Class. Thanks to his close involvement in the testing-and-development program for this model range, Wangler knows the G-Class as no one else does. As a result, the 1989 European off-road trials champion was sent around the world by Mercedes-Benz as a G-Class "technical advisor," to instruct the most diverse group of customers.

Mercedes-Gelaendewagenclub.de

■ G-Club Aachen

There are active and less active G clubs. In Aachen you can really rightly speak of very active G-Class drivers, because the group from Charlemagne's imperial city organizes several off-road events a year. In addition to regular trips to the North African Sahara, there are the gatherings at the large gravel pit near Grevenbroich, Germany, where, in addition to a few ML, a good fifty Mercedes G drivers—from the 280 GE built in 1979 to the new W 463 A—always find their gathering to drive together the highlight of the year. Apart from the so-called free driving, the participants can also try their hand at specially marked trial sections.

■ Mercedes G Club UK

In England, fans of the G-Class had a hard time for a long time. From 1996 to 1998, there were no right-hand-drive G models available. Nevertheless, a strong association of interested people formed there, named the G Wagen Owners Association (GWOA). In Great Britain. the contact person is David J. Watkins.

■ GWOA
gwoa.co.uk/

■ Switzerland
Swiss G-Club
swiss-g-club.ch/

■ United States
Club G-Wagen
clubgwagen.com/

■ France
Club MBF
clubmbf.com/

■ The Netherlands
MB G-Klasse Club Nederland
mbgcn.nl

■ Club Mercedes G Italia
clubmercedesg.it/

■ Mercedes G-Club Czech Republic
mb-g.cz/

■ Club Mercedes G España
clubmercedesg.es/

■ Mercedes-Benz SUV Club of Southern Africa
gwagenclub.co.za/

■ The G-Class on the internet

G-club-ev.de
G-Wagen.co.uk/
mercedes-benz.com
G-Wagen.com/
gwagen.com
g-class.ru
GFG-4x4.de
tschiewagon.com
g-classics.com
desert-service.com
schmude-hardtop.de
G-Wagen.eu
g-raid.de
vikingoffroad.com
Viermalvier.de
offroad-forum.de
hanshehl.de
4x4ABC.com
ORC.de
lennartz-technik.de
S-Tec.at
Puch.at
Mercedes-Benz-G.at
mercedes-benz.de/G-Klasse
gw-gelaendewagen.de
4x4kiefer.de

■ G-Class addresses

Mercedes-Benz
Mercedesstr. 1, 70546 Stuttgart, Germany
Tel.: +49 (0) 711-17-0
Mercedes-Benz.com

MBGTC GmbH
Mercedes-Benz Gebrauchtteile Center
Mörikestr. 60-64, 73765 Neuhausen, Germany
Tel.: +49 (0) 711-17 70 000
mbgtc.de

Mercedes AMG GmbH
Daimlerstr. 1, 70546 Affalterbach, Germany
Tel.: +49 (0) 7144-302-0
Mercedes-Benz.com/AMG.com

Brabus Autosport
Brabusallee 1, 46240 Bottrop, Germany
Tel.: +49 (0) 2041-777-0
Brabus.com

ORC
Robert-Bosch-Strasse 14, 71088 Holzgerlingen, Germany
Tel.: +49 (0) 7031-209280
ORC.de

Magna-Steyr-Daimler-Puch
Fahrzeugtechnik AG & CoKG
Liebenauer Hauptstrasse 317, A-8041 Graz, Austria
styer-daimler-puch.com

MKB Motorenbau GmbH
Otto-Hahn-Strasse 2, 71364 Winnenden, Germany
Tel.: +49 (0) 7195-9161-0
mkb-power.de

GFG mbH
Gewerbegebiet 15,
99894 Leinatal OT Schönau v.d. Walde, Germany
Tel.: +49 (0) 36253-477545
G-Raid.de

G Wagon Car Technology GmbH
Hauptstr. 111, A-8580 Rosental an der Kainach, Austria
Tel: +43 (0) 664-9110361
tschiewagon.com

GZR
Hauptstr. 2, 29365 Sprakensehl, Germany
Tel.: +49 (0) 5837-140033

g-manufaktur.de

LeTech
Ruitzenmühle 12, 71364 Winnenden, Germany
Tel.: +49 (0) 7195-9576611
Lennartz-Technik.de

MGS-Geländewagentechnik
Bönninghardter Str. 68i, 46519 Alpen, Germany
Shop@MGS-4x4.de

S-Tec
Frank Stronach Straße 3, A-8200 Albersdorf,
Austria
Tel: +43 (0) 3112-90000

s-tec.at

G-Shop
Wiesenstraße 9, 56479 Niederroßbach, Germany
Tel.: +49 (0) 151-72040600
g-shop24.de

Offroad World
Hauptstraße 15, 22929 Rausdorf, Germany
Tel.: +49 (0) 4154-6398
offroad-world.com

Thanks

First of all, I would like to thank my wife, Annika, for her support. At Daimler AG, I would like to particularly thank Christian Anosowitsch, their Mercedes G-Class press contact person. I would like to thank GFG mbH and Auto Zitzmann for the opportunities for the photo shoots; Hans Hehl and Michael Steiger for their additional input; the Mercedes G-Clubs in Germany, Switzerland, and the Netherlands for the opportunity to do research at events; Stefan Commertz; and last but not least, of course thanks to HEEL Verlag, especially Jost Neßhöver and Jürgen Schlegelmilch.

Images

Daimler AG, GFG mbH, ORC GmbH, Jörg Sand, Alexander Kirsch, Hans-Joerg Schekahn, Robb Pritchard, Gordon Arthur, Daniel Wiesel, Peter Majole, G-Club NL, Swiss G-Club, Mercedes G-Club e.V., Martin Breuniger, Marc Bote, Carl Schulze, Claws Thosche, Michael Steiger, Hans Hehl, Hans Kiefer, Dr. Björn Schulz, Stephan Pees, Peter Guttormsen, Mercedes G-Club Aachen, GORM/German Off-Road Masters, Mercedes AMG GmbH, Brabus GmbH, Karl Volger, *Mercedes G-Wagen Magazin* international 2009–2019, the Bundeswehr Archive, CM Pro Photo.

Literature

Breuninger, Martin. *Das G-Buch* ("The G book"). Radolfzell, Germany: TUFA Verlag, 1995.

Breuninger, Martin. *Das G-Reisebuch*. Radolfzell, Germany: TUFA Verlag, 1995.

Breuninger, Martin. *Die Legende fährt weiter: 25 Jahre Mercedes G-Klasse*. Radolfzell, Germany: TUFA Verlag, 2004.

Flügeling, Michael. *Das große Mercedes G-Buch* ("The big Mercedes G book"). Munich: AC Verlag, 1996.

Joubert, Jan. *4×4: A Practical Guide to Off-Road Adventures in Southern Africa*. Cape Town: Struik Verlag, 1999.

Taylor, Blaine. *Mercedes-Benz Parade and Staff Cars of the Third Reich*. Barnsley, UK: Pen and Sword Books, 1999.